Daily Skill Builders:
Word Problems

By
LINDA ARMSTRONG

COPYRIGHT © 2008 Mark Twain Media, Inc.

ISBN 978-1-58037-446-0

Printing No. CD-404087

Mark Twain Media, Inc., Publishers
Distributed by Carson-Dellosa Publishing Company, Inc.

Table of Contents

Introduction to the Teacher iv
NCTM Standards Matrix for Grades 5–8 1

Activity #   Skill

1. Find Facts, Locate Questions, and Select Processes 1
2. Find Facts, Locate Questions, and Select Processes 1
3. Place Value 2
4. Place Value 2
5. Addition: Three Digits, No Regrouping........... 3
6. Addition: Three Digits, No Regrouping........... 3
7. Subtraction: Three Digits, No Regrouping....... 4
8. Subtraction: Three Digits, No Regrouping........ 4
9. Addition: Two and Three Numbers, Three Digits With Regrouping 5
10. Addition: Two and Three Numbers, Three Digits With Regrouping 5
11. Subtraction With Regrouping 6
12. Subtraction With Regrouping 6
13. Mixed Addition and Subtraction 7
14. Mixed Addition and Subtraction 7
15. Round Off to Tens and Hundreds 8
16. Round Off to Tens and Hundreds 8
17. Estimating 9
18. Estimating 9
19. Multiplication: One-Digit Times Two-Digits 10
20. Multiplication: One-Digit Times Two-Digits 10
21. Multiplication With Regrouping 11
22. Multiplication With Regrouping 11
23. Division: One-Digit Divisor, No Remainder 12
24. Division: One-Digit Divisor, No Remainder 12
25. Division: One-Digit Divisor With Remainder... 13
26. Division: One-Digit Divisor With Remainder... 13
27. Division: One-Digit Divisor, Three-Digit Dividend, No Remainder.............................. 14
28. Division: One-Digit Divisor, Three-Digit Dividend, No Remainder.............................. 14
29. Division: One-Digit Divisor, Three-Digit Dividend With Remainder 15
30. Division: One-Digit Divisor, Three-Digit Dividend With Remainder 15
31. Checking Division With Multiplication 16
32. Checking Division With Multiplication 16
33. Division: Two-Digit Divisors 17
34. Division: Two-Digit Divisors 17
35. Averages.. 18
36. Averages.. 18
37. Averages.. 19
38. Averages.. 19
39. Identifying Polygons, Lines, Line Segments, and Rays.. 20
40. Identifying Polygons, Lines, Line Segments, and Rays.. 20
41. Identifying Right Angles, Acute Angles, and Obtuse Angles 21
42. Identifying Right Angles, Acute Angles, and Obtuse Angles 21
43. Identifying the Radius and Diameter of a Circle 22
44. Identifying the Radius and Diameter of a Circle 22
45. Symmetry... 23
46. Symmetry... 23
47. Identifying Congruent Figures........................ 24
48. Identifying Congruent Figures........................ 24
49. Identifying Fractions.. 25
50. Identifying Fractions.. 25
51. Comparing Fractions Using a Fraction Bar Chart 26
52. Comparing Fractions Using a Fraction Bar Chart 26
53. Recognizing Equivalent Fractions Using a Chart... 27
54. Recognizing Equivalent Fractions Using a Chart... 27
55. Generating Equivalent Fractions.................... 28
56. Generating Equivalent Fractions.................... 28
57. Adding Fractions 29
58. Adding Fractions 29
59. Subtracting Fractions 30
60. Subtracting Fractions 30
61. Reducing Proper and Improper Fractions...... 31
62. Reducing Proper and Improper Fractions...... 31
63. Changing Mixed Numbers to Improper Fractions 32
64. Changing Mixed Numbers to Improper Fractions 32
65. Adding and Subtracting Mixed Numbers 33
66. Adding and Subtracting Mixed Numbers 33
67. Recognizing Decimal Fractions 34
68. Recognizing Decimal Fractions 34
69. Adding and Subtracting Decimal Fractions.... 35
70. Adding and Subtracting Decimal Fractions.... 35
71. Comparing Decimals and Fractions............... 36
72. Comparing Decimals and Fractions............... 36
73. Line Graphs.. 37
74. Bar Graphs... 37
75. Pie Graphs.. 38
76. Pie Graphs.. 38
77. Probability 39
78. Probability 39
79. Ordered Pairs... 40

Table of Contents (cont.)

80. Ordered Pairs.................................. 40
81. Tree Diagrams and Probability..................... 41
82. Tree Diagrams and Probability..................... 41
83. Measurement: Length—Inches, Feet, and Yards 42
84. Measurement: Length—Inches, Feet, and Yards 42
85. Measurement: Length—Up to a Meter 43
86. Measurement: Length—Up to a Meter 43
87. Measurement: Length—Foot to Mile............. 44
88. Measurement: Length—Foot to Mile............. 44
89. Measurement: Length—Meter to Kilometer ... 45
90. Measurement: Length—Meter to Kilometer ... 45
91. Perimeter and Area................................ 46
92. Perimeter and Area................................ 46
93. Volume... 47
94. Metric Volume 47
95. Measurement: Weight—Ounces and Pounds 48
96. Measurement: Weight—Ounces and Pounds 48
97. Measurement: Weight—Grams and Kilograms 49
98. Measurement: Weight—Kilograms and Metric Tons 49
99. Elapsed Time 50
100. Elapsed Time 50
101. Speed and Distance 51
102. Speed and Distance 51
103. Time Zones 52
104. Time Zones 52
105. Money 53
106. Money 53
107. Money: Estimation 54
108. Money: Estimation 54
109. Money: Adding and Subtracting.................... 55
110. Money: Adding and Subtracting.................... 55
111. Money: Multiplying 56
112. Money: Multiplying 56
113. Money: Dividing 57
114. Money: Dividing 57
115. Basic Operations With Numbers More Than 1,000....................................... 58
116. Basic Operations With Numbers More Than 1,000....................................... 58
117. Three-Digit Divisors.............................. 59
118. Three-Digit Divisors.............................. 59
119. Range, Median, and Mean 60
120. Range, Median, and Mean 60
121. Adding and Subtracting Unlike Fractions 61
122. Adding and Subtracting Unlike Fractions 61

123. Adding and Subtracting Mixed Numbers 62
124. Adding and Subtracting Mixed Numbers 62
125. Multiplying Mixed Numbers: Area 63
126. Multiplying Mixed Numbers: Area 63
127. Dividing Fractions 64
128. Dividing Fractions 64
129. Multiplying With Decimal Fraction Multipliers 65
130. Multiplying With Decimal Fraction Multipliers 65
131. Dividing With Decimal Fraction Divisors 66
132. Dividing With Decimal Fraction Divisors 66
133. Percents 67
134. Percents 67
135. Ratios 68
136. Ratios 68
137. Proportions 69
138. Proportions 69
139. Three-Dimensional Forms 70
140. Three-Dimensional Forms 70
141. Circumference.................................... 71
142. Circumference.................................... 71
143. Areas of Triangles 72
144. Areas of Complex Shapes 72
145. Pictographs 73
146. Pictographs 73
147. Surveys 74
148. Surveys 74
149. Coordinate Graphing 75
150. Logic Problems 75
151. Integers.. 76
152. Surface Area of Rectangular Solids.............. 76
153. Calculating Interest 77
154. Multiple Line Graphs 77
155. Equations With Missing Operations 78
156. Venn Diagrams 78
157. Add and Round Off Large Numbers 79
158. Multiply and Round Off Decimals 79
159. Exponents 80
160. Reducing Fractions 80
161. Changing Fractions to Decimals 81
162. Factor Trees 81

Answer Keys.. 82

Introduction to the Teacher

To solve word problems effectively, students must determine what is being asked, locate relevant information, and decide which operation to perform before they carry out any calculations. The same comprehension skills that support students in literature, history, and science are essential for solving word problems in math. While making students more aware of the practical applications of mathematics in their daily lives, guided practice with word and logic problems can help them become more focused readers.

The question is the heart of any word problem. It is easy, but ultimately frustrating, to waste precious time and energy chasing down the answer to a question that was not asked. After skimming the material, students should imagine that they are detectives and make sure they understand what their "client" wants to know. Encourage them to ferret out question words and phrases.

For example, the question might ask "Which boy is the fastest?" Although students would use an operation involving numbers to solve the problem, the answer to the question would be a name.

Sample question words and phrases:

How many	*How far*	*How long*	*Which*	*What time*
What	*Who*	*Where*	*Why*	

With the question in mind, students need to determine which information is relevant. In most textbook problems, all of the information offered will be used in some way, but in the real world, this is not true. As a result, test-makers often include extra facts in their paragraphs. Students should read carefully and select only the information that will help them find the answer.

Once they have isolated relevant facts, problem-solvers must select the proper operation. Certain words are often clues.

Sample clue words and phrases:	Operation Required:
• *in all*	addition or multiplication
• *all together*	addition or multiplication
• *how many more than*	subtraction
• *how much larger than*	subtraction
• *to the nearest*	rounding off or estimation
• *about*	estimation
• *of*	multiplication of fractions
• *how many _____ are there in*	division

Daily Skill Builders: Word Problems is designed to increase students' ability to use math effectively in their schoolwork as well as in their everyday lives. As students develop their knowledge and understanding of grammatical usage, punctuation, and capitalization, their ability to comprehend the word problems, effectively solve them, and then communicate the answers verbally and in writing will also improve.

Encourage students to use dictionaries, thesauruses, and other reference sources when working on activities. After all, a student can't use a word correctly if he or she does not know its meaning.

Introduction to the Teacher (cont.)

Topics Covered

The activities in this book focus on skills that enable students to:

- use mathematical operations in everyday situations;
- determine questions, find relevant facts, and select appropriate operations;
- estimate results and check their own calculations;
- unleash the real-world power of place value;
- gather and interpret data;
- create drawings, diagrams, and other models to solve problems;
- perform basic, practical operations with fractions and decimals;
- reduce fractions to their lowest terms and convert them to their decimal equivalents;
- understand the importance of equivalence when working with proportions, ratios, fractions, and basic equations;
- perform operations with U.S. standard and/or metric measures of length, weight, and volume;
- perform basic operations with money;
- work with elapsed time, speed, distance, and differences between time zones;
- use ordered pairs of integers to locate points on a map, graph, or axis;
- read and/or generate bar graphs, pie graphs, line graphs, and pictographs;
- use information presented in Venn diagrams to solve problems;
- recognize the properties of lines, shapes, and forms;
- find the perimeters of polygons;
- use formulae to find the perimeter of a circle and the area of a triangle;
- solve problems requiring more than one operation; and
- solve logic problems.

Suggestions for Use

Each activity page is divided into two reproducible sections that can be cut apart and used separately. Activities could be used in class as warm-ups or for review either with a group or individually. Transparencies of the activities can encourage student participation as they follow along when a new concept is introduced. Extra copies can be kept in your learning center for review and additional practice, or copies can be distributed as homework assignments.

Organization

Activities are arranged by skill level and topic and are progressively more difficult. Later activities build on knowledge covered earlier in the book.

Since reading comprehension and the use of reasoning are skills being assessed in most state and national standardized tests, this book will help students master those skills.

The table of contents identifies the skills that students use to complete each activity. An answer key is provided at the end of the book. A matrix of skills addressed by each activity, based on NCTM standards, is also included.

NCTM Standards Matrix for Grades 5–8

Problem Solving

- Build new mathematical knowledge through problem solving—**Level 1:** 1–56; **Level 2:** 57–112; **Level 3:** 113–62

- Solve problems that arise in mathematics and in other contexts—**Level 1:** 1–56; **Level 2:** 57–112; **Level 3:** 113–62

- Apply and adapt a variety of appropriate strategies to solve problems—**Level 1:** 1–56; **Level 2:** 57–112; **Level 3:** 113–62

- Monitor and reflect on the process of mathematical problem solving—**Level 1:** 1, 2, 13, 14, 21, 25, 30, 33, 34, 55, 56; **Level 2:** 60, 65, 66, 71, 72, 77–82, 87, 88, 90–8, 103–110; **Level 3:** 116, 117, 119, 120, 123, 124, 126, 139, 140, 142, 144, 148–51, 155, 156, 161, 162

Reasoning and Proof

- Recognize reasoning and proof as fundamental aspects of mathematics—**Level 1:** 1, 2, 17, 18, 20, 21, 23, 24, 31, 32, 35, 38, 44–7, 49–52, 54, 56; **Level 2:** 57–9, 63–6, 69–72, 77–82, 85, 93, 94, 98, 101, 102, 105–8; **Level 3:** 119, 120, 123, 124, 139, 140, 142, 144, 147–51, 161

- Make and investigate mathematical conjectures—**Level 1:** 15–8, 20, 21, 23, 24, 31, 32, 35, 38, 44–7, 49–52, 56; **Level 2:** 57–9, 62–6, 69–72, 77–82, 85, 93, 94, 98, 101, 102, 105–8; **Level 3:** 119, 120, 123, 124, 139, 140, 142, 144, 147, 148, 151, 155, 161

- Develop and evaluate mathematical arguments and proofs—**Level 1:** 17, 18, 20, 21, 23, 24, 31, 32, 35, 38, 44–7, 49–52, 56; **Level 2:** 59, 65, 66, 69–72, 77–82, 85, 93, 94, 98, 101, 102, 105–8; **Level 3:** 119, 120, 123, 124, 139, 140

- Select and use various types of reasoning and methods of proof—**Level 1:** 17, 18, 20, 21, 23, 24, 31, 32, 35, 38, 44–7, 49–52, 56; **Level 2:** 59, 65, 66, 69–72, 77–82, 85, 93, 94, 98, 101, 102, 105–8; **Level 3:** 119, 120, 123, 124, 139, 140, 142, 144, 147, 148, 151, 155, 161

Communication

- Organize and consolidate mathematical thinking through communication—**Level 1:** 1–4, 13, 14, 17, 18, 35–50, 53, 54; **Level 2:** 57, 59, 61–8, 73–98, 107, 108; **Level 3:** 119–149, 151–4, 156, 159, 160, 162

- Communicate mathematical thinking coherently and clearly to peers, teachers, and others—**Level 1:** 1–4, 13, 14, 35–50, 53, 54; **Level 2:** 57, 59, 61–70, 73, 74, 77–98, 107, 108; **Level 3:** 119–54, 156, 159, 160, 162

- Analyze and evaluate the mathematical thinking and strategies of others—**Level 1:** 1–4, 15 ,16, 35–50, 53–6; **Level 2:** 57, 59, 61–8, 77–82, 93, 94; **Level 3:** 119, 120, 123, 124, 139, 140, 147–50

- Use the language of mathematics to express mathematical ideas precisely—**Level 1:** 1–4, 13–8, 35–8, 41–50, 53–6; **Level 2:** 57, 59, 61–70, 73–98, 107, 108; **Level 3:** 119–49, 151–4, 156, 159, 160, 162

Connections

- Recognize and use connections among mathematical ideas—**Level 1:** 13–8, 21, 31, 32, 47, 48, 55, 56; **Level 2:** 81–98, 101–6, 109–12; **Level 3:** 113–8, 121–34, 139, 140, 143, 144, 152–5, 157, 158, 160, 161

- Understand how mathematical ideas interconnect and build on one another to produce a coherent whole—**Level 1:** 13–8, 21, 31, 32, 35–8, 47, 47, 48, 53–6; **Level 2:** 57–66, 69, 70, 81–98, 101–12; **Level 3:** 113–8, 121–34, 139, 140, 143, 144, 152–5, 157, 158, 160, 161

- Recognize and apply mathematics in contexts outside of mathematics—**Level 1:** 1–56; **Level 2:** 57–112; **Level 3:** 113–62

Representation

- Create and use representations to organize, record, and communicate mathematical ideas—**Level 1:** 9, 13–20, 22, 35–48, 51–5; **Level 2:** 67–70, 73–6, 79, 80, 85–8, 90–2, 95, 98-104, 107–12; **Level 3:** 113, 114, 116, 119, 120, 125, 126, 129, 130, 133–137, 139, 140, 144, 147–152, 154, 156, 157, 162

- Use representation to model and interpret physical, social, and mathematical phenomena—**Level 2:** 73, 74, 103, 104; **Level 3:** 113, 114, 116, 119, 120, 125, 126, 129, 130, 133–137, 139, 140, 144–152, 154, 156, 157, 162

ACTIVITY 1 Find Facts, Locate Questions, and Select Processes

Name:_____

Date:_____

To solve a word problem, first find the facts and decide what is being asked. Read the paragraph, and answer the questions.

Scientists discover four lines of spiny lobsters traveling across the sea floor. There are 62 lobsters in one line, 60 lobsters in another line, 56 lobsters in the third line, and 59 lobsters in the last line.

1. What number facts are given? _____

2. What is being counted? _____

3. Write a question that asks for a total amount, and then add to answer it. _____

_____

4. Write a question that asks for a difference, and then subtract to answer it._____

_____

ACTIVITY 2 Find Facts, Locate Questions, and Select Processes

Name:_____

Date:_____

The same group of facts may be used to create several different problems. Try it!

The rhinoceros iguana, which lives on the island of Hispaniola, lays up to 20 eggs in a burrow. While studying an iquana colony, naturalists found 12 eggs in the first burrow, 6 eggs in the second burrow, 11 eggs in the third burrow, and 20 eggs in the fourth burrow.

1. What number facts are given? _____

_____

2. What is being counted? _____

3. Write a question that asks for a comparison. _____

_____

4. Write a question that asks for a total. Then solve the problem. _____

_____

5. Write a question that asks for a difference. Then solve the problem. _____

_____

ACTIVITY 3 Place Value

Name:_____

Date:_____

When is a one not a one? A one in the thousands place stands for one thousand, and a one in the hundreds place stands for one hundred. Read the problem and answer the questions.

Chris is changing his town's population sign. Slots in the back of the sign are marked for the ones, tens, hundreds, thousands, and ten thousands places. Chris must slide the correct number card into each place. The town's current population is 234,169.

1. Which number will he enter in the ten-thousands place?
   _____

2. Which number will he enter in the tens place?
   _____

3. Which number will he enter in the hundred-thousands place?
   _____

4. Which number will he enter in the hundreds place? _____

5. Which number will he enter in the thousands place? _____

ACTIVITY 4 Place Value

Name:_____

Date:_____

Use place value to answer the questions.

Mary likes to garden. She puts one plant in the first row, two plants in the second row, and so on. She has a total of 17 rows in her garden. Answer the following questions about Mary's garden.

1. Mary grew two pumpkin plants. In which row were the pumpkins? _____

2. Peppers were in row 12. How many pepper plants did Mary have? _____

3. Mary loves fresh corn most of all. What is the biggest number of corn plants she could grow?
   _____

4. Watermelons were in row 5. How many watermelon plants did Mary need to buy?
   _____

5. Mary grew two kinds of tomato plants: paste tomatoes in row 7, and beefsteak tomatoes in row 8. Which kind of tomato did she plant more of? _____

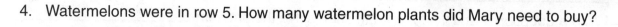

ACTIVITY 5 Addition: Three Digits, No Regrouping

Name:_____

Date:_____

Gather the facts and then add. Keep the ones, tens, and hundreds lined up.

Kara's team earned 324 points in her school's community service competition. Jared's team earned 223 points, Jason's team earned 101 points, and Mike's team earned 452.

1. How many points did Mike's team and Jason's team earn in all?

    _____

2. How many points did Kara's team and Jason's team earn in all?

    _____

3. How many points did Jason's team and Jared's team earn in all? _____

4. How many points did Kara's team and Mike's team earn in all? _____

5. Which pair earned 675 points? _____

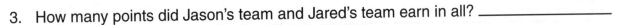

ACTIVITY 6 Addition: Three Digits, No Regrouping

Name:_____

Date:_____

Read about the school's aluminum can drive, and then answer the questions.

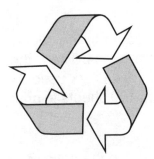

Leo collected 730 aluminum cans during his club's recycling drive. Jeremy collected 265. Gerardo brought in 620. Jordan gathered 532, and Miguel turned in 614.

1. How many cans did Leo and Jeremy collect in all?

    _____

2. How many cans did Gerardo and Jordan turn in?

    _____

3. How many cans did Leo and Miguel turn in? _____

4. How many cans did Jeremy and Gerardo collect? _____

5. Which pair collected 797 cans? _____

3

ACTIVITY 7) Subtraction: Three Digits, No Regrouping

Name:_____

Date:_____

Read the paragraph and answer the questions in order.

The public library's computer keeps track of returns. On Saturday morning, 478 books were due. By 11:30 A.M., 200 of them had been returned. By 1:30, another 150 had been returned. When the library closed at 6:00 P.M., only 10 books were still due.

1. How many books were still due at 11:30 A.M.? _____

2. How many books were still due at 1:30 P.M.? _____

3. How many books were returned between 1:30 P.M. and 6:00 P.M.? _____

_____

4. How many of the books that were due were returned on Saturday? _____

_____

ACTIVITY 8) Subtraction: Three Digits, No Regrouping

Name:_____

Date:_____

Read this paragraph about the school office and solve the subtraction problems. Check your work by adding.

On Monday morning, there were 958 sheets of white paper in the supply room. The office manager used 122 sheets to print a notice. Then, the nurse used 203 sheets to print permission slips. Next, Mrs. Clark used 21 sheets to print a history test. Finally, the counselor used 100 sheets to print a Career Day survey.

1. How many sheets of white paper were left after the office manager printed the notice?

_____

2. How many sheets were left after the nurse printed the permission slips?

_____

3. How many sheets were left after Mrs. Clark printed the history test?

_____

4. How many sheets were left after the counselor printed the Career Day survey?

_____

ACTIVITY 9 **Addition: Two and Three Numbers, Three Digits With Regrouping**

Name:_____

Date:_____

Check Dr. Martin's chart and answer the questions. You will need to regroup.

Dr. Martin was studying wolf spider families. He caught four mother wolf spiders and counted the baby spiders they were carrying on their backs.

Spider Moms	
Spider	No. of Babies
Spider A	89
Spider B	96
Spider C	77
Spider D	108

1. How many baby spiders were spider moms A, B, and C carrying? _____

2. How many babies were spider moms B, C, and D carrying? _____

3. How many babies were spider moms A, B, and D carrying? _____

4. How many babies were all four spider moms carrying? _____

ACTIVITY 10 **Addition: Two and Three Numbers, Three Digits With Regrouping**

Name:_____

Date:_____

Read about Myra's photography and answer the questions. You will need to regroup.

Myra wants to be a photographer. Each month, she takes as many digital pictures as she can. In January, she took 65 pictures. In February, she shot 183. In March, she took 246 pictures. In April, she took 89, and in May, she took 294.

1. How many pictures did Myra take in January, February, and March?

   _____

2. How many pictures did she take in February, March, and April?

   _____

3. How many pictures did Myra take in her three busiest months?

   _____

4. How many pictures did she take in her three slowest months?

   _____

ACTIVITY 11 | Subtraction With Regrouping

Name:_____

Date:_____

Read the paragraph and answer the questions. You will need to regroup.

Kyle belongs to a stamp collecting club. He has 835 international stamps in his albums. Carter, a beginner, has 19 stamps. Davis has 626 stamps. Edgar has 553, and Alvin has 97.

1. Carter would like to have as many stamps as Kyle. How many more does he need? _____

2. Edgar will soon have as many stamps as Davis. How many more does he need? _____

3. How many more stamps does Edgar have than Alvin?

   _____

4. Davis and Kyle showed their collections at a regional stamp exposition. How many more stamps does Kyle have than Davis? _____

ACTIVITY 12 | Subtraction With Regrouping

Name:_____

Date:_____

Check the facts. Read each question carefully before answering. You will need to regroup.

As a recycling project, Vanessa's class collected plastic bottles. On Monday, the students collected 88 bottles. On Tuesday, they collected 192. On Wednesday, they brought in 253. On Thursday, they gathered 215, and on Friday, they collected 185.

1. On Monday, the students did not bring in very many bottles. How many more did they bring in on Tuesday than on Monday?

   _____

2. On Wednesday, they brought in the most bottles. How many fewer did they bring on Thursday? _____

3. They brought in 88 bottles on Monday. How many more did they bring in on Friday than on Monday? _____

4. They brought in more bottles on Thursday than they did on Friday. How many more?

   _____

ACTIVITY 13 Mixed Addition and Subtraction

Name: _____

Date: _____

Add or subtract? You decide. Check the facts and read each question carefully.

On December 31, Baker's Beans donated 500 cans of each type of bean to the Lamar Food Bank.

1. How many cans of garbanzo beans have been given away? _____

2. How many cans of kidney beans, chili beans, and garbanzo beans are left all together?

   _____

3. How many cans of black beans have been given away?

   _____

4. How many cans of navy beans and black beans are left?

   _____

Cans Remaining in Stock as of February 1

Cans of kidney beans	456
Cans of garbanzo beans	263
Cans of black beans	397
Cans of navy beans	421
Cans of chili beans	299

ACTIVITY 14 Mixed Addition and Subtraction

Name: _____

Date: _____

Find the clue words that tell you whether to add or subtract. Underline them, and then answer the questions.

1. How many more tomatoes than zucchinis were sold? _____

2. How many onions, tomatoes, and bunches of cilantro were sold in all? _____

3. How many potatoes and tomatoes were sold in all? _____

4. How many more bunches of cilantro than onions were sold? _____

Weekend Farm Stand Sales

potatoes	107
tomatoes	292
zucchini	163
onions	67
bunches of cilantro	276

ACTIVITY 15 **Round Off to Tens and Hundreds**

Name:_____

Date:_____

Rounding can help you estimate answers quickly. If the number in the ones place is 5 or more, round the number in the tens place up. If the number in the tens place is 5 or more, round the number in the hundreds place up.

Example: 253 would be rounded to 300, and 243 would be rounded to 200.

1. A marketer mailed out magazine subscription offers to about 8,400 people in Hesterville. According to the data table, were the offers for *Sports' Day, Lady's Life, Active Girl,* or *Today's Boy*? _____

2. The recreation center sent fliers to about 8,220 people. Did the fliers advertise a women's retreat or a men's golf tournament?
_____

3. The parents of about 680 children buy clothing in local stores. Do they shop for them in the boys' department or the girls' department? _____

POPULATION OF HESTERVILLE

Men	8,219
Women	8,386
Girls	634
Boys	677

ACTIVITY 16 **Round Off to Tens and Hundreds**

Name:_____

Date:_____

Use the information in the chart to answer the questions. Round off.

1. Clear book jacket covers come in sets of ten. How many covers did the librarian order for the books in the nonfiction section? _____
How many did she order for the picture book section?
_____

2. A bookcase holds one hundred books. How many new bookcases did the librarian order for the fiction section?
_____
How many did she order for the picture book section?
_____

3. Jake's favorite section has about 130 books. Which section is it? _____

4. Ray told his mom there were about 900 nonfiction books and 100 reference books in the library. How many fiction books did he say there were? _____

Dorian Street School Library

Nonfiction	915
Fiction	552
Reference	131
Picture books	456
Easy readers	234

ACTIVITY 17 Estimating

Name: _____

Date: _____

Round off and add to answer these questions about record-breaking waterfalls.

1. Which two falls, together, would be about 6,000 feet tall?

_____

2. Which two falls, together, would be about 5,300 feet tall?

_____

3. Which falls is about 300 feet taller than Monge Falls?

_____

4. Would the height of the three falls, together, be closer to 8,000 feet or 9,000 feet? _____

Highest Waterfalls in the World

Waterfall	Height in Feet
Angel Falls in Venezuela	3,212
Tugela Falls in South Africa	2,800
Monge Falls in Norway	2,540

ACTIVITY 18 Estimating

Name: _____

Date: _____

Round off and subtract to compare the world's great rivers.

1. Which river is about 1,100 km longer than the Huang He? _____

2. Which river is about 2,000 km shorter than the Nile? _____

3. Which river is about 200 km shorter than the Chang Jiang? _____

4. Which river is about 700 km longer than the Ob? _____

Longest Rivers in the World

River	Length
Nile River, Egypt	6,689 km long
Amazon River, South America	6,296 km long
Chang Jiang River, China	5,797 km long
Ob River, Russia	5,567 km long
Huang He River, China	4,667 km long

ACTIVITY 19 Multiplication: One Digit Times Two Digits

Name:_____

Date:_____

Multiply to answer these parking lot problems.

1. Which parking lot has 280 cars?

   _____

2. How many cars are in Parking Lot D?

   _____

3. Which parking lot has the fewest cars?

   _____

4. How many cars are in Parking Lot B?

   _____

Parking Lot A: 5 rows of 11 cars
Parking Lot B: 8 rows of 21 cars
Parking Lot C: 7 rows of 40 cars
Parking Lot D: 3 rows of 22 cars

ACTIVITY 20 Multiplication: One Digit Times Two Digits

Name:_____

Date:_____

Business people use multiplication every day. Check the information, and then answer the questions.

Mr. Dustin, a local farmer, is ready for the weekly produce market. His truck is loaded with fruit.

1. How many pears are in the truck? _____
2. Mrs. Carter is planning to make jam. She will buy all of the boxes of one kind of fruit. There will be 189 fruits in all. What kind of jam is she making?

   _____

3. If Mr. Melvin needs 50 apples for the school vending machines, will he be able to buy all of them from Mr. Dustin today? _____
4. How many apricots are on the truck? _____

Mr. Dustin's Harvest

Boxes of Fruit	Pieces of Fruit per Box
9 boxes of peaches	21 per box
5 boxes of pears	30 per box
2 boxes of apples	24 per box
3 boxes of apricots	52 per box

ACTIVITY 21   Multiplication With Regrouping

Name:_____

Date:_____

Sometimes, there is more than one way to find an answer. You could use repeated addition to answer these questions, but multiplication is faster and more accurate.

Diana and her friends made woven place mats for the Honor Roll Luncheon. For each place mat, they needed 6 strips of red paper and 9 strips of orange paper. They made 58 mats. They also made award certificates. On each certificate, they placed 7 gold stars and 5 silver stars. The certificates were awarded to 39 students.

1. How many strips of red paper did the girls use?

   _____

2. How many strips of orange paper did the girls use?

   _____

3. How many gold stars did they use? _____

4. If there were 200 silver stars in a box, was one box of silver stars enough, or did they open a second one? _____

ACTIVITY 22   Multiplication With Regrouping

Name:_____

Date:_____

Read the paragraph, check the chart, and answer the questions.

Every fifth-grade student in Lakeside School District planted five tree seedlings in the mountains after a large forest fire. Every sixth-grade student planted six trees. Every seventh-grade student planted seven trees, and every eighth-grade student planted eight trees.

1. How many trees did the eighth graders plant?

   _____

2. How many trees did the fifth graders plant?

   _____

3. The sixth graders grew 1,800 seedlings. Was that enough? _____

4. How many trees did the seventh graders plant?

   _____

Number of Students in Lakeside School District	
Grade 5	364
Grade 6	299
Grade 7	309
Grade 8	277

ACTIVITY 23 Division: One-Digit Divisor, No Remainder

Name:_____

Date:_____

For each problem, there are 72 legs. Use division to solve these leggy riddles.

1. Ladybird beetles each have six legs. How many ladybird beetles would there be? _____

2. Beagles have four legs each. How many beagles would there be? _____

3. With two legs each, how many basketball players would there be? _____

4. If there were two horses on a team, and all horses had four legs each, how many teams of horses would there be? _____

ACTIVITY 24 Division: One-Digit Divisor, No Remainder

Name:_____

Date:_____

Math and food are natural partners. Use division to solve these problems. There are 90 raisins for each problem.

1. If oatmeal cookies needed nine raisins each, how many cookies could you make?

_____

2. If the recipe called for five raisins for each scoop of carrot salad, how many scoops could you make?

_____

3. If there were three raisins in each spoonful of bran cereal, how many spoonfuls would you have?

_____

4. If you were using two raisins to make faces on your pancakes, how many faces could you make?

_____

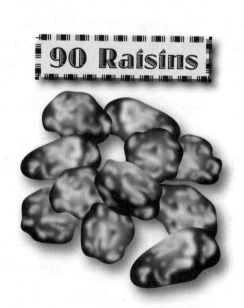

ACTIVITY 25 Division: One-Digit Divisor With Remainder

Name:_____

Date:_____

Sometimes, drawing pictures helps to solve problems. To answer one of these questions, draw the bags on your own paper and use circles to stand for the apples. Use division to answer the others.

There are 93 apples.

1. A farmer places the apples in 5 evenly-filled bags. How many apples are in each bag? _____ How many are left over? _____

2. A shipper places the apples in three boxes filled with an even number of apples. How many apples are in each box? _____ How many apples are left over? _____

3. Laura and Deb make candy apples for the fall carnival. They sell their treats in pairs. How many candy apple pairs do they make? _____ How many apples are left over? _____

4. Mrs. Crawford makes pies for a scholarship fund-raiser. She uses four apples to make each pie. How many pies does she make? _____ How many apples are left over? _____

ACTIVITY 26 Division: One-Digit Divisor With Remainder

Name:_____

Date:_____

How would this bookstore divide up an important shipment? Read each question carefully. There will be remainders.

There are 89 books.

1. Copies of a best seller arrive at Downtown Books in 8 evenly-filled boxes. The remainder of the shipment is included in a padded envelope. How many books are in each box? _____ How many are in the envelope? _____

2. Most of the books are stored on two shelves in the back room. They are divided equally. How many books are on each shelf? _____
How many are left over? _____

3. Exactly nine books are sold each day. On which day is the last full batch of nine books sold: the eighth day, the ninth day, or the tenth day? _____

4. How many books are left on the last day? _____

ACTIVITY 27 Division: One-Digit Divisor, Three-Digit Dividend, No Remainder

Name:_____

Date:_____

Read the paragraph and divide to answer the questions.

Two hundred pieces of trash were collected in Mason Park on Saturday morning. Eight service club members collected all of the litter. Each member collected the same number of pieces.

1. How many pieces of trash did each member collect? _____

2. Equal amounts of trash were placed in four plastic bags. How many pieces of trash were placed in each bag? _____

3. Equal amounts of trash were carried to the dump in two vans. How many pieces of trash were carried in each van? _____

4. The club earned one service point for each five pieces of trash collected. How many service points did the club receive? _____

ACTIVITY 28 Division: One-Digit Divisor, Three-Digit Dividend, No Remainder

Name:_____

Date:_____

Read the facts, and then divide to answer the questions.

Purple Pencil Company donated 344 pencils to the sixth graders at Larson School.

1. If each sixth grader received 4 pencils and none were left over, how many sixth graders were there at Larson School? _____

2. If the pencils were shipped in two equally-packed boxes, how many pencils were in each box? _____

3. If the pencils were packaged in eight bags, how many pencils were in each bag? _____

4. How many bags of pencils were packed in each box? _____

ACTIVITY 29 Division: One-Digit Divisor, Three-Digit Dividend With Remainder

Name: _____

Date: _____

Read the facts and divide to answer the questions.

A new movie theater in town wanted to attract business. They sent 2,561 free passes to Cherry Hill School.

1. Each student received 5 free passes; how many students attended the school?

   _____

2. How many passes were left over? _____

3. Most of the passes came in packets of four. How many packets were sent? _____

4. How many passes were not included in a packet?

   _____

ACTIVITY 30 Division: One-Digit Divisor, Three-Digit Dividend With Remainder

Name: _____

Date: _____

Sometimes, remainders can answer questions. Solve these division problems.

Adventure Park wanted to promote Thursday as Family Night. They printed up 1,735 coupons good for one free game of kid's mini golf with the purchase of one adult game of mini golf.

1. Adventure Park mailed each family 3 coupons. How many families got coupons?

   _____

2. How many coupons were left over? _____

3. 107 families used all three coupons. How many coupons were used by these families? _____

4. 282 families used two of the three coupons. How many coupons were used by these families? _____

5. 96 families used only one coupon. How many coupons were used by these families?

   _____

6. Of those coupons mailed, how many coupons were not used? _____

ACTIVITY 31 Checking Division With Multiplication

Name:_____

Date:_____

An easy way to check a division problem is to multiply the quotient by the divisor. If there is a remainder, add it to the product. The result should be the dividend.

When Jared organized his sports card collection, he realized he had duplicate cards. He decided to divide the 210 extra sports cards among five of his friends.

1. How many cards would each of his friends receive? _____

2. Before counting out the cards, Jared multiplied to be sure that he had divided them equally. Write the multiplication problem Jared used. _____

3. One of Jared's friends decided he did not want any cards, so Jared divided them into four sets instead. How many cards would be in each new set? How many would be left over? _____

4. Write the multiplication problem Jared used to check his division.

_____

ACTIVITY 32 Checking Division With Multiplication

Name:_____

Date:_____

Read the paragraph and answer the questions.

Cindy made cupcakes for her little brother's birthday party. She bought a bagful of round, colorful candies to decorate them. When she counted, Cindy discovered that there were 205 candies. She wanted to put five candies on each cupcake.

1. How many cupcakes could she decorate? _____

2. Before Cindy made the cupcakes, she wrote a multiplication problem to make sure she had the right number. Write that problem here. _____

3. When she heard that fewer children would be coming to the party, Cindy decided to place seven candies on each cupcake, instead. How many cupcakes could she decorate? How many candies would be left over? _____

4. Write the multiplication problem Cindy used to check her division.

_____

ACTIVITY 33 Division: Two-Digit Divisors

Name:_____

Date:_____

At the annual Founder's Day picnic, Mark and Jason helped the recreation director organize some activities. Divide to answer these questions.

1. First, the boys separated 204 children into twelve equal teams for relay races. How many children were on each team?

   _____

2. Next, they prepared crafts materials. To assemble necklace kits, they divided 900 beads into sets with 25 beads each. How many kits did they make? _____

3. At lunchtime, they helped 180 children find their places at 15 tables. If the boys separated the children into equal groups, how many were seated at each table? _____

4. In the afternoon, Mark and Jason divided 170 children into 34 clusters for small-group nature activities. How many children were in each cluster?

   _____

- -

ACTIVITY 34 Division: Two-Digit Divisors

Name:_____

Date:_____

Divide to solve these seating problems.

1. When it is full, the cafeteria seats 238 students. Each table seats 14 students. How many tables are there in the cafeteria? _____

2. There are 154 students in the cafeteria and equal numbers are sitting at 14 tables. How many students are sitting at each table? _____

3. There are 176 students in the cafeteria. The same number of students is sitting at each of 11 tables. How many students are sitting at each table? _____

4. There are 90 students in the cafeteria. The same number of students is sitting at each of 15 tables. How many students are sitting at each table? _____

ACTIVITY 35   Averages

Name:_____

Date:_____

To find the average of a group of numbers, add them together, and then divide by the number of addends.
For example, to find the average of 4, 2, and 3, add 4 + 2 + 3 = 9.
Then divide 9 by 3, or 9 ÷ 3 = 3.

Kenneth's soccer team, the Westdale Tigers, played ten games during the season. Here are their scores.

1. What was the average score in the first five games?
   _____

2. What was the average score in the second five games? _____

3. What was the average score in the last three games?
   _____

4. Did the team improve over the season or get worse?
   _____

Westdale Tigers Season Scores

Game	Score	Game	Score
Game 1	6	Game 6	4
Game 2	1	Game 7	4
Game 3	2	Game 8	3
Game 4	1	Game 9	5
Game 5	5	Game 10	4

- -

ACTIVITY 36   Averages

Name:_____

Date:_____

Compare the math team's scores. Average facts from the chart to answer the questions.

Miguel's math team competed in four regional competitions. Here are the team's scores.

	Miguel	Davis	Barb	Abe	Dennisha
Meet 1	88	80	90	92	90
Meet 2	82	95	81	89	93
Meet 3	90	85	89	95	91
Meet 4	80	90	90	90	100

1. What was the average score for all five team members in Meet 4? _____

2. What was Miguel's average score for all four meets? _____

3. What was Davis's average score for all four meets? _____

4. What was the average score of all five team members in Meet 1? _____

ACTIVITY 37 Averages

Name: _____

Date: _____

Use the information in the chart to find the averages.
Shade the bubble beside each correct answer.

The students in Adam's study group kept track of their weekly geography test scores.

	Kara	Austin	Chase	Adam
Test 1	81	81	90	92
Test 2	77	73	81	89
Test 3	72	67	89	80
Test 4	70	60	86	92
Test 5	80	69	84	87

1. What was Kara's average score for all five tests?

   (a.) 72   (b.) 76   (c.) 84   (d.) 69

2. What was Austin's average score for all five tests?

   (a.) 69   (b.) 70   (c.) 90   (d.) 88

3. What was Chase's average score for all five tests?

   (a.) 81   (b.) 74   (c.) 81   (d.) 86

4. What was Adam's average score for all five tests?

   (a.) 88   (b.) 90   (c.) 68   (d.) 72

ACTIVITY 38 Averages

Name: _____

Date: _____

Check the facts and answer the questions.

Jake, Edgar, and Mark wanted to join the basketball team, but their grades were too low, so they formed a support group. For the first month, they helped each other study science and kept track of their scores.

	Jake	Edgar	Mark
Quiz 1	92	90	87
Quiz 2	89	92	88
Quiz 3	80	78	82
Quiz 4	92	84	83
Quiz 5	87	76	80

1. What was Edgar's average score for all five quizzes? _____

2. What was Mark's average score for all five quizzes? _____

3. What was the group's average score for quiz 3? _____

4. What was the group's average score for quiz 5? _____

5. Before forming the group, the boys' average quiz score was 64. Did they improve? To what? _____

ACTIVITY 39 **Identifying Polygons, Lines, Line Segments, and Rays**

Name:_____

Date:_____

A **line** is a collection of points extending in two directions with no end points. A **ray**, part of a line, has one endpoint. A **line segment** is part of a line with two endpoints. A **polygon** is a closed two-dimensional shape with three or more sides. Use these definitions and the diagrams to answer the questions.

 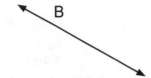 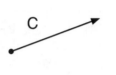

Sengel Point lived on Planet Todimentia, an odd place where everything disappears if viewed from the side. One morning, Sengel could not find her sister, Ann Other.

1. First, she looked on the local line segment. Did she go to A, B, C, or D? _____

2. Next, she went to the polygon. Was it A, B, C, or D? _____

3. Ann was nowhere to be seen, so Sengel visited the line. Was it A, B, C, or D? _____

4. Finally, she found Ann on the ray. Was it A, B, C, or D? _____

ACTIVITY 40 **Identifying Polygons, Lines, Line Segments, and Rays**

Name:_____

Date:_____

Here is a challenge! Use clues to name the homes of Todimentia's inhabitants. Circle the correct answer.

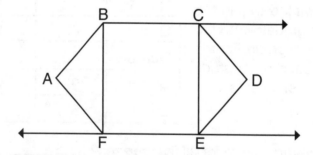

1. Dot Point's home is ABF. It is a (triangle / rectangle / hexagon).

2. Won Dot's home is FBCE. It is a (triangle / rectangle / hexagon).

3. A. Place lives on ABCDEF. It is a (triangle / rectangle / hexagon).

4. R. Spot is part of BC. It is a (polygon / line / ray).

5. Trudy Point lives on FE. That is a (triangle / line / line segment / ray).

ACTIVITY 41 **Identifying Right Angles, Acute Angles, and Obtuse Angles**

Name:_____

Date:_____

Acute angles are less than 90 degrees. **Right angles** are 90 degrees, and **obtuse angles** are greater than 90 degrees. Study the diagrams and circle the correct answers.

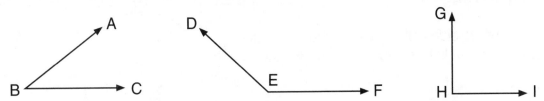

1. The shape of Lara's first initial is an angle. It is a(n) (right / acute / obtuse) angle.
2. When Charlie draws the profile of a bird, he uses an angle for the beak similar to ∠ABC. It is a(n) (right / acute / obtuse) angle.
3. When Mike draws a picture of his house, he uses an angle for the roof similar to ∠DEF. It is a(n) (right / acute / obtuse) angle.
4. A square has four angles. They are (right / acute / obtuse) angles.

ACTIVITY 42 **Identifying Right Angles, Acute Angles, and Obtuse Angles**

Name:_____

Date:_____

Angles have names. The letter in the middle labels the vertex. Each of the other letters labels a point on one of the sides. Study the diagram and circle the correct answers.

When Catherine drew a picture of her home's roof, she used many angles.

1. Angle BAG is a(n) (right / acute / obtuse) angle.
2. Angle FBE is a(n) (right / acute / obtuse) angle.
3. Angle BED is a(n) (right / acute / obtuse) angle.

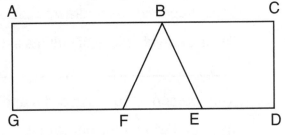

4. How many acute angles are there in Catherine's picture? _____
5. How many obtuse angles are there in the picture? _____
6. How many right angles are there in the picture? _____

ACTIVITY 43   Identifying the Radius and Diameter of a Circle

Name: _____

Date: _____

The **radius** is a line segment connecting the center of a circle to a point on the circle. The **diameter** is a line segment that passes through the center of a circle and has both of its end points on the circle. The **circumference** is the perimeter of a circle. Study the diagram and answer the questions.

When Becky used sidewalk chalk to draw a four-square court for her little sister, she labeled these points.

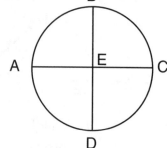

1.   Is EB the radius, the diameter, or the circumference? _____

2.   Is AC the radius, the diameter, or the circumference? _____

3.   Is point E the center, the radius, or the circumference? _____

4.   EC is one radius of this circle. Name three others. _____

ACTIVITY 44   Identifying the Radius and Diameter of a Circle

Name: _____

Date: _____

Jason drew a mystery shape with chalk. He told his brother to hold a broomstick very still. He tied one end of a piece of string to the broomstick and a piece of sidewalk chalk to the other end. He pulled the string tight and placed the chalk on the pavement. He kept the string tight and walked around the broomstick, drawing a line as he went.

1.   What shape did Jason draw? _____

2.   Was the straight piece of string a side, an angle, a radius, a diameter, or a circumference?

_____

3.   Every person in your class is standing exactly the same distance from you. What is the

shape and what is the name of the spot where you are standing? _____

_____

4.   If a computer started to draw all the possible diameters of a circle, how many would there

be? _____

ACTIVITY 45 Symmetry

Name:_____

Date:_____

After answering the questions, try cutting out some letters.

Anna is cutting out letters for a bulletin board. She has discovered that she can make some letters by folding and cutting. This is because some letters are symmetrical.

1. Circle the letters that are not symmetrical. On the symmetrical letters, draw lines to show planes of symmetry. These planes of symmetry will be Anna's fold lines. (Hint: Where would you place a mirror on half of the letter to make it look whole?)

A B C D E F G H I J K L M N O P Q R S T U V W X Y Z

2. When the gray areas are cut away, and the paper is unfolded, which letter will Anna see? _____

3. Draw a pattern for a folded letter Y in the box to the right. Color the cut-away section gray.

ACTIVITY 46 Symmetry

Name:_____

Date:_____

After answering the questions, design a logo for your own screen name.

Mark Matthews is designing a personal logo for his web site. The logo uses both of his initials. It has two planes of symmetry.

1. Finish Mark's logo.

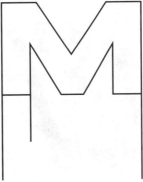

2. Design a logo for Emily Ellenwood.

ACTIVITY 47   Identifying Congruent Figures

Name:_____

Date:_____

Congruent shapes may be turned, or oriented, in different directions, but they match in every other way. Study the diagrams and answer the questions.

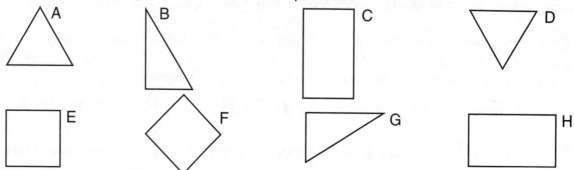

Jan, Kara, Jordan, and Martin are making shape books.

1. One of Jan's covers is A. What is her other cover? _____

2. Kara's covers are also triangles. Which ones are they? _____, _____

3. One of Jordan's covers is H. What is the other? _____

4. One of Martin's covers is E. What is the other? _____

ACTIVITY 48   Identifying Congruent Figures

Name:_____

Date:_____

Tony is assembling a spaceship control panel for his nephew. Metal pieces fit into special slots. Help Tony by identifying the congruent shapes. Study the panel and the pieces, and then answer the questions.

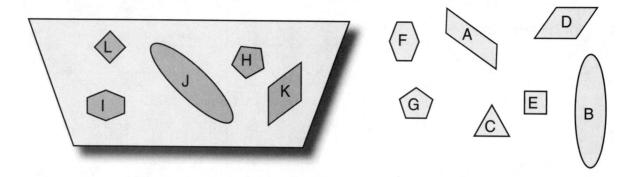

1. Which shape fits into slot J? _____   2. Which shape fits into slot L? _____

3. Which shape fits into slot K? _____   4. Circle the shapes that do not fit in the panel.

ACTIVITY 49 Identifying Fractions

Name:_____

Date:_____

The **numerator** (the top number in a fraction) tells how many parts are being described. The **denominator** (the number on the bottom) shows how many parts there are in all. Study the information below and answer the questions. Draw pictures on your own paper if you wish.

Abby is making a chart with information about Martin Junior High's eighth grade class. She illustrates the following facts:

1. Abbie draws a circle divided into seven equal parts. How many of those parts does she color in? _____ Which fact is she illustrating? _____

2. Abbie draws a rectangle divided into six equal parts. How many of the parts does she color in? _____ Which fact is she illustrating? _____

3. Abbie draws a rectangle, divides it into equal parts, and colors in three of those parts. Which fact is she illustrating? _____

4. Abbie draws a circle, divides it into equal parts, and colors in seven of those parts. Which fact is she illustrating? _____

A. Seven-eighths of the students eat in the school cafeteria at least one day a week.

B. Five-sevenths of the students plan to attend college.

C. Three-fifths of the students enjoy athletic events.

D. Five-sixths of the students use the school library.

ACTIVITY 50 Identifying Fractions

Name:_____

Date:_____

Be a fraction detective. Use these clues to identify the items and write the fractions. Match the fractions to their descriptions.

A.    B.    C.    D.    E.

1. Seven green apples in a basket with five red apples _____

2. Two green chocolate buttons in a bowl with thirteen red chocolate buttons _____

3. Nine yellow pencils in a box with one blue pencil _____

4. Four white erasers in a drawer with thirteen gray erasers _____

5. Five red paper clips in a bag with four blue paper clips _____

ACTIVITY 51 **Comparing Fractions Using a Fraction Bar Chart**

Name:_____

Date:_____

Read the paragraph. Use the fraction bar chart to answer the questions.

Allen's class helped to plant a community garden. Each student was given a packet with the same number of seeds. Allen planted $\frac{9}{16}$ of his seeds. Grace planted $\frac{1}{2}$ of her seeds. Armando planted $\frac{4}{5}$ of his seeds, and Bill planted $\frac{5}{6}$ of his seeds.

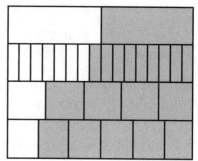

1. Who planted the most seeds? _____
2. Who planted the fewest seeds? _____
3. Who planted more seeds, Allen or Grace? _____
4. Who planted more seeds, Armando or Allen? _____

Challenge: Who ended the session with an equal number of planted and unplanted seeds?

_____

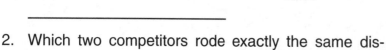

ACTIVITY 52 **Comparing Fractions Using a Fraction Bar Chart**

Name:_____

Date:_____

Read the paragraph. Use the fraction bar chart to answer the questions.

Jeremy, Heather, Liv, and Marcus participated in a charity bike ride. In the first hour of the ride, Jeremy finished $\frac{3}{8}$ of the course, Heather finished $\frac{4}{10}$, Liv finished $\frac{2}{5}$, and Marcus finished $\frac{3}{6}$ of the course.

1. Who traveled the greatest distance in the first hour?

_____

2. Which two competitors rode exactly the same distance? _____

3. Which competitor completed exactly $\frac{1}{2}$ of the course?

_____

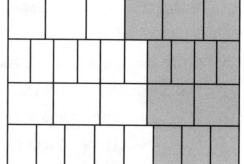

4. If the riders keep traveling at the same rate, how much longer will it take for Marcus to reach the finish line? _____

26

ACTIVITY 53 Recognizing
Equivalent Fractions Using a Chart

Name: _____

Date: _____

Read the paragraph, and then label the days of the week and write the fractions on the chart.

Day   **Fraction**

_____   _____

_____   _____

_____   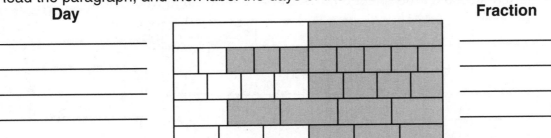   _____

_____   _____

_____   _____

On Monday, $\frac{8}{10}$ of Mrs. Carson's class joined in discussion. Tuesday, half spoke up. Wednesday, $\frac{3}{6}$ of the students took part. Thursday, $\frac{4}{8}$ participated, and on Friday, $\frac{4}{5}$ joined the discussion.

1. On which days did only $\frac{1}{2}$ of the students participate in the class discussion?

    _____, _____, _____

2. On which days did $\frac{4}{5}$ of the students take part? _____,

    _____

- -

ACTIVITY 54 Recognizing
Equivalent Fractions Using a Chart

Name: _____

Date: _____

Read the clues, and then write the girl's name and the fraction of cups she can fill across from the correct shaded bar. One has been done for you.

Name	Fraction
_____	_____
Carol	$\frac{4}{16}$
_____	_____
_____	_____
_____	_____

Carol and her friends are selling cold drinks at the game. Each girl has an identical pitcher and a stack of differently sized cups. A pitcher will fill 16 of Carol's cups, 12 of Anna's cups, and 10 of Laura's cups. A pitcher will also fill 6 of Geneva's cups, 4 of Mariah's, and 3 of Jamaica's.

1. Carol filled 4 cups. That was $\frac{4}{16}$ of the lemonade in her pitcher. Anna used the same amount of lemonade. How many cups did she fill? _____

2. Laura filled five cups. That was $\frac{5}{10}$ of her lemonade. Mariah used the same amount of lemonade. How many cups did she fill? _____

27

ACTIVITY 55   Generating Equivalent Fractions

Name:_____

Date:_____

Use the clues to shade in the fraction bars that have not already been shaded, and write in the missing equivalent fractions for the shaded parts showing how much was eaten.

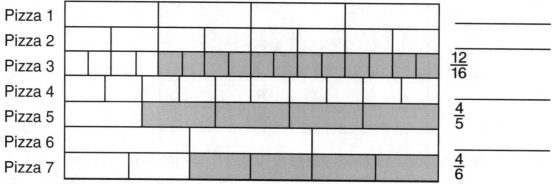

Pizza 1 _____

Pizza 3 $\frac{12}{16}$

Pizza 4 _____

Pizza 5 $\frac{4}{5}$

Pizza 7 $\frac{4}{6}$

Nathan brought 7 pizzas to share with his class. The shaded sections show how much of pizzas 3, 5, and 7 were eaten at the party. The same amounts of pizzas 1, 2, and 3 were eaten. The same amounts of pizzas 4 and 5 were eaten. The same amounts of pizzas 6 and 7 were eaten.

1. What fraction of pizza 1 was left? _____ Of pizza 2? _____

    Of pizza 3? _____ Are these fractions equivalent? _____

ACTIVITY 56   Generating Equivalent Fractions

Name:_____

Date:_____

Reminder: To create an equivalent fraction, multiply both the numerator and the denominator of a fraction by the same number.

Gabe, Kenyon, and Abe hold a contest. When Gabe says "go," the boys start writing equivalent fractions for $\frac{3}{4}$.

1. Kenyon likes to work in order. After $\frac{3}{4}$, he writes $\frac{6}{8}$. When Gabe says "stop," Kenyon is writing $\frac{30}{40}$. Fill in the blanks in Kenyon's list: $\frac{6}{8}$, _____, _____, _____,

    _____, _____, _____, _____, $\frac{30}{40}$.

2. Gabe likes to work in multiples of ten. After $\frac{3}{4}$, he writes $\frac{30}{40}$. When he says "stop," Gabe is writing $\frac{300}{400}$. Fill in the blanks in Gabe's list: $\frac{30}{40}$, _____, _____, _____,

    _____, _____, _____, _____, $\frac{300}{400}$.

3. After $\frac{3}{4}$, Abe writes $\frac{15}{20}$. Then, he writes $\frac{30}{40}$, and then $\frac{45}{60}$. He continues to follow that pattern. What are his next two numbers? _____, _____

ACTIVITY 57 Adding Fractions

Name:_____

Date:_____

When adding like fractions, add only the numerators.
The denominators remain the same.

When Jason surveyed his class, he discovered that $\frac{7}{28}$ of the students wanted to go to the beach for the year-end picnic and $\frac{5}{28}$ wanted to have the picnic at the city pool. He found that $\frac{12}{28}$ wanted to take a hike in the mountains, and $\frac{4}{28}$ wanted to go to the movies.

1. What fraction of the class wanted to have the class picnic near water?

    _____

2. What fraction of the class wanted to have the end-of-the-year activity

    outdoors? _____

3. What fraction of the class did not want to have the picnic near water?

    _____

4. If the decision was made according to the majority's choice, what fraction of the class

    might be unhappy? _____

ACTIVITY 58 Adding Fractions

Name:_____

Date:_____

Many recipes use fractions. Read about Marlene's nut-free
trail mix and answer the questions.

Marlene made nut-free trail mix for the class hike. The measuring cup she used was marked in 32nds. She included $\frac{7}{32}$ raisins, $\frac{10}{32}$ rice crackers, $\frac{5}{32}$ dried bananas, and $\frac{10}{32}$ pretzel pieces.

1. What fraction of the trail mix was sweet? _____

2. What fraction of the trail mix was salty? _____

3. What fraction of the trail mix did not include raisins? _____

4. What fraction of the trail mix did not include rice crackers? _____

29

ACTIVITY 59 Subtracting Fractions

Name:_____

Date:_____

Reminder: When subtracting like fractions, consider only the numerators. The denominators remain the same.

Karen made salad dressing. The vinegar bottle contained $\frac{7}{8}$ of a cup. She poured $\frac{1}{8}$ cup of that into a mixing bottle. Her olive oil bottle contained $\frac{5}{8}$ of a cup, and she poured $\frac{2}{8}$ cup of that into the mixing bottle. She added crushed garlic, a little water, some salt, some sugar, and a pinch of dried basil. When Karen finished, her mixing bottle contained $\frac{4}{8}$ of a cup of dressing. After shaking the mixture, she poured $\frac{3}{8}$ of a cup over fresh greens and tossed the salad.

1. After Karen poured vinegar into her mixing bottle, how much was left in the vinegar bottle? _____
2. After Karen poured olive oil into her mixing bottle, how much was left in the oil bottle? _____
3. After Karen poured dressing on the salad, how much was left in the mixing bottle? _____
4. Did Karen have enough vinegar and olive oil to make another batch of dressing? _____

ACTIVITY 60 Subtracting Fractions

Name:_____

Date:_____

Read the paragraph and answer the questions in order.

At the town's SummerFest picnic, Ms. Carter cut a melon into 24 pieces and placed the slices on a serving table. Just as she finished, members of the dog parade group stopped by. They ate $\frac{11}{24}$ of the melon slices. Next, the volunteer firefighters arrived. They ate $\frac{10}{24}$ of the slices. After the firefighters left, Ms. Carter's children ate $\frac{2}{24}$ of the slices.

1. What fraction of the melon remained after the dog parade group left? _____
2. What fraction of the melon remained after the firefighters left? _____
3. What fraction of the melon remained after Ms. Carter's children finished snacking? _____

ACTIVITY 61 Reducing Proper and Improper Fractions

Name:_____

Date:_____

To change an improper fraction to a mixed number, divide the numerator by the denominator. The quotient is the whole number, and the remainder is the numerator of the fraction part of the mixed number.

Mrs. Demetri sells fresh eggs by the dozen at her farm stand. There are 12 eggs in a dozen, so 14 eggs can be written as $\frac{14}{12}$ or $1\frac{1}{6}$ dozen.

1. 26 eggs = $\frac{26}{12}$ of a dozen or _____ dozen.

2. 18 eggs = $\frac{18}{12}$ of a dozen or _____ dozen.

3. 39 eggs = $\frac{39}{12}$ of a dozen or _____ dozen.

4. 8 eggs = $\frac{8}{12}$ of a dozen or _____ dozen.

ACTIVITY 62 Reducing Proper and Improper Fractions

Name:_____

Date:_____

Read the example, and then fill in each missing mixed number.

Jacob fixes computer problems for customers on an hourly basis. He saves the money he earns for college. There are 60 minutes in an hour, so 90 minutes is the same as $\frac{90}{60}$ of an hour, or $1\frac{1}{2}$ hours.

1. 65 minutes = $\frac{65}{60}$ of an hour, or _____ hours.

2. 128 minutes = $\frac{128}{60}$ of an hour, or _____ hours.

3. 99 minutes = $\frac{99}{60}$ of an hour, or _____ hours.

4. 45 minutes = $\frac{45}{60}$ of an hour, or _____ hour.

ACTIVITY 63 Changing Mixed Numbers to Improper Fractions

Name:_____

Date:_____

To change a mixed number to an improper fraction, multiply the whole number by the denominator, and add the numerator. The resulting number is the new numerator.

Waterfall Acres Campground is very popular. The owners charge visitors by the day and by any fraction of a day that they stay. There are 24 hours in a day, so 1 day and 2 hours is $\frac{26}{24}$ of a day. What fraction of a day are the following times?

1. 2 days and 4 hours = _____ of a day.

2. 1 day and 6 hours = _____ of a day.

3. 3 days and 1 hour = _____ of a day.

4. 1 day and 8 hours = _____ of a day.

ACTIVITY 64 Changing Mixed Numbers to Improper Fractions

Name:_____

Date:_____

Study the paragraph. Change the mixed numbers to improper fractions.

Becky works in her mother's fabric store on weekends. She measures a lot of ribbon, which is sold by the yard. There are 36 inches in a yard, so 1 yard and 3 inches is $\frac{39}{36}$ of a yard. What fraction of a yard are the following lengths?

1. 3 yards 5 inches is _____ of a yard.

2. 2 yards 10 inches is _____ of a yard.

3. 4 yards 2 inches is _____ of a yard.

4. 5 yards 1 inch is _____ of a yard.

ACTIVITY 65 **Adding and Subtracting** Name:_____
Mixed Numbers Date:_____

To add or subtract mixed numbers, keep the whole numbers lined up according to place value. If regrouping is necessary, remember that one whole equals a fraction with the same numerator and denominator.

1. On Saturday, Andy and David went on a hike. They packed $1\frac{1}{2}$ cheese and $1\frac{1}{2}$ chicken sandwiches. How many whole sandwiches did the boys take with them? _____

2. They walked $1\frac{1}{4}$ km, and rested for 30 minutes. Afterwards, they walked another $1\frac{2}{4}$ km. They ate lunch beside a waterfall. Then, they walked back to the start of the trail. How far did they walk to get to the waterfall? _____
   How far did they walk in all? _____

3. The boys were gone for $3\frac{3}{4}$ hours. They spent $1\frac{1}{4}$ hours eating lunch. How long did they spend walking? _____

4. It took the boys $1\frac{1}{2}$ hours to reach the waterfall. How long did it take them to hike back to the trailhead? _____ Which way do you think was uphill? Give a reason for your answer. _____

ACTIVITY 66 **Adding and Subtracting** Name:_____
Mixed Numbers Date:_____

Read about Kaila's road trip, and then add or subtract to answer the questions.

Kaila's family took a trip to three national parks. The first day, everyone packed the car. It took $2\frac{3}{4}$ hours. Then, they drove for $3\frac{3}{4}$ hours before stopping to eat. After lunch, they drove for another $4\frac{1}{4}$ hours before stopping at a motel.

1. If family members ate breakfast just before packing, how many hours was it before they ate again? _____

2. In total, how many hours did they drive? _____

3. If they spent $1\frac{1}{4}$ hours eating lunch, how many hours was it from the time they started packing until they stopped for the day? _____

4. If they started packing at 6 A.M., what time did they arrive at the motel?

_____

ACTIVITY 67 **Recognizing Decimal Fractions**

Name:_____

Date:_____

Decimal fractions are based on multiples of ten.

Examples: The decimal fraction 0.1 is equal to the fraction $\frac{1}{10}$; $0.01 = \frac{1}{100}$; and $0.001 = \frac{1}{1000}$.

Sarah's committee created a chart for their class report. Sarah's job is to write a decimal fraction for each shaded part of each bar in the chart. Study the charts and write the decimal fractions.

1. ▭▭▭▭▭▭▭▭▭▭ _____

2. ▭▭▭▭▭▭▭▭▭▭ _____

3. ▭▭▭▭▭▭▭▭▭▭ _____

4. 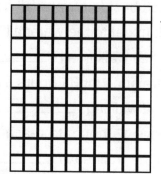 _____

- -

ACTIVITY 68 **Recognizing Decimal Fractions**

Name:_____

Date:_____

Reminder: The decimal fraction 0.1 is equal to the fraction $\frac{1}{10}$; $0.01 = \frac{1}{100}$; and $0.001 = \frac{1}{1000}$.

Jason's father designs and installs tile floors. Last summer, Jason helped him write orders for tile. It was Jason's job to write the decimal fraction for the shaded part of each diagram. Write the decimal fractions below.

1.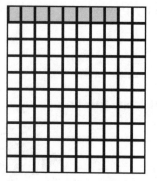

2.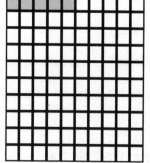

3.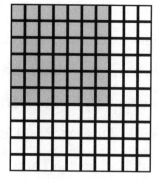

_____   _____   _____

ACTIVITY 69 Adding and Subtracting Decimal Fractions

Name:_____

Date:_____

Adding and subtracting decimal fractions is like any other addition or subtraction. Line up the decimal points according to place value.

Alden has model trains. He is putting together a freight train. The length of each car is listed in the table.

Type of Car	Length (in cm)
tank car	10.2
flat car	15.7
refrigerator car	13.4
caboose	7.6

1. Alden adds only one of each type of car to his train. How long is it? _____

2. He adds three more tank cars to his train. Now how long is it? _____

3. The engine breaks down on the hill. Alden decides to remove the refrigerator car to lighten the load. Now how long is his train? _____

4. If he does some switching on his train and leaves the flat car on the side, how long is his train? _____

ACTIVITY 70 Adding and Subtracting Decimal Fractions

Name:_____

Date:_____

Reminder: Include the decimal point in your answer when adding or subtracting decimal fractions.

Book Title	Weight (in kg)
The Universe	1.81
Twenty Incredible Stories	1.94
Insects of the World	1.88
Endangered Animals	2.04

Gracie is putting books into her backpack. The pack's instructions warn not to carry more than 6.65 kilograms at once. The books Gracie wants to carry and how much they weigh are listed in the table.

1. If Gracie puts all of the books in her backpack, how much will it weigh? _____

2. How much over the pack's weight limit would that be? _____

3. If she removes *Twenty Incredible Stories*, how much would the remaining books weigh?

_____

4. If she puts *Twenty Incredible Stories* back in and removes *Endangered Animals* instead, how much would the remaining books weigh? _____

ACTIVITY 71 Comparing Decimals and Fractions

Name:_____

Date:_____

Reminder: When comparing decimals to fractions, 0.2 is the same as $\frac{2}{10}$ or $\frac{1}{5}$.

Carson and Danny are brothers. After a swim in the local pool, the boys go to the sandwich shop for a snack. Carson offers to give Danny a portion of his order. Danny is hungry, and he does not want his brother to trick him.

1. Should he choose $\frac{1}{2}$ or 0.4 of the sandwich? _____

2. Which should he choose, $\frac{1}{4}$ or 0.1 of the fries? _____

3. Should he choose $\frac{1}{6}$ or 0.6 of the drink? _____

4. Which should he choose, $\frac{2}{3}$ or 0.7 of the cookie?

_____

ACTIVITY 72 Comparing Decimals and Fractions

Name:_____

Date:_____

Reminder: 0.25 is the same as $\frac{25}{100}$ or $\frac{1}{4}$.

Rebecca wants to be the next student body president.

1. Would she rather receive 0.25 or $\frac{1}{3}$ of the boys' vote? _____

2. Would she rather receive 0.75 or $\frac{2}{3}$ of the girls' vote? _____

3. Would she rather receive 0.8 or $\frac{18}{20}$ of the seventh-grade vote? _____

4. Would she rather receive 0.67 or $\frac{7}{12}$ of the total vote? _____

ACTIVITY 73 Line Graphs

Name: _____

Date: _____

Study the graph and answer the questions.

1. What was the warmest day of the week?

_____

2. What were the coldest days of the week?

_____

3. How much warmer was it on Tuesday than

on Friday? _____

4. What was the average temperature for the

week? _____

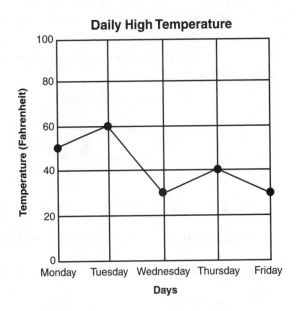

Daily High Temperature

ACTIVITY 74 Bar Graphs

Name: _____

Date: _____

Study the graph and answer the questions.

1. Which candidate received the most votes?

_____

2. Which candidate received the fewest votes?

_____

3. How many more votes did Laura receive than

Denise? _____

4. How many votes were cast in all?

_____

5. What was the average number of votes

received per candidate? _____

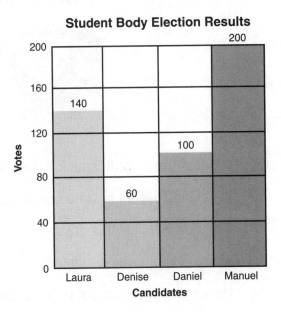

Student Body Election Results

ACTIVITY 75 Pie Graphs

Name:_____

Date:_____

Pie graphs allow you to compare facts easily. The entire circle represents 100% of the results. Study the graph and answer the questions.

Favorite Sandwiches at Mesa Park Middle School

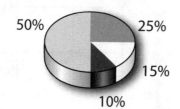

50%   25%

15%

10%

50% Prefer Grilled Cheese
25% Prefer Roast Turkey
10% Prefer Sliced Beef
15% Prefer Peanut Butter

1. What is the favorite kind of sandwich at Mesa Park Middle School? _____

2. What is the least favorite kind of sandwich? _____

3. Do more students prefer roast turkey or peanut butter? _____

4. The numbers on the graph represent percentages. If 200 students answered the survey question, how many students chose grilled cheese? _____

ACTIVITY 76 Pie Graphs

Name:_____

Date:_____

Study the graph and answer the questions.

Favorite Snacks at Hillside School

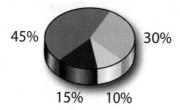

45%   30%

15%   10%

45% Prefer Apples
30% Prefer Bananas
10% Prefer Ants On A Log
15% Prefer Trail Mix

1. What is the favorite snack at Hillside School? _____

2. What is the least favorite snack? _____

3. The numbers on this graph represent percentages. If 100 students took the survey, how many of them chose apples? _____

4. How many more students preferred apples than preferred trail mix? _____

ACTIVITY 77 Probability

Name: _____

Date: _____

To find the probability of a certain outcome, compare the number of target items to the total number of items. Write the two numbers in this form: 5:10.

A velvet bag contains 10 gems. There are 4 sapphires, 3 diamonds, 2 emeralds, and 1 ruby. Reach into the bag and pull out a stone.

1. What is the probability of pulling out a ruby? _____

2. What is the probability of pulling out a sapphire? _____

3. What is the probability of pulling out an emerald? _____

4. What is the probability of pulling out a diamond? _____

5. What is the probability of not pulling out a ruby? _____

Challenge: Test the probability in real life! Use stones or marbles in place of the gems. Put the "gems" back and shake the bag after each draw.

ACTIVITY 78 Probability

Name: _____

Date: _____

Have you ever wondered what chance you really have of winning a prize? Find out how many tickets will be sold, and then compare that information to the number of tickets you plan to purchase.

Example: You buy six tickets in a raffle. 3,396 tickets were sold. You would write that as 6:3,396. You could then reduce that to 1:566. That means you have a one in 566 chance of winning the raffle.

The Marine Science Club is holding a lottery to raise money for a trip to the aquarium. When the drawing is held, they have sold exactly 250 tickets. The prize is a fish tank and four fish.

1. Andrea buys 12 tickets. What is the probability that she will win the prize?

    _____

2. Ryan buys 17 tickets. What is the probability that he will not win the prize?

    _____

3. Madison buys 25 tickets. What is the probability that she will not win the prize?

    _____

4. Alex buys 50 tickets. What is the probability that he will win the prize? _____

ACTIVITY 79   Ordered Pairs

Name:_____

Date:_____

Study the graph and answer the questions. In an ordered pair, the first number identifies the number of lines to the right (or left) of the vertex, and the second number identifies the number of lines above (or below) the vertex.

1. Jonathan's pet parakeet flew out the window. It flew to (1, 2). Where did it land?

_____

2. Then, it flew to (3, 4). On what did it land?

_____

3. Next, it flew to (4, 3). On what did it land?

_____

4. What did it find at (5, 3)?

_____

5. Jonathan finally found it at (4, 1). Was it beside a fence, in a park, or under a telephone pole?

_____

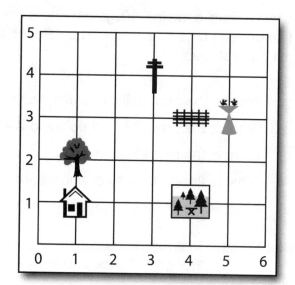

ACTIVITY 80   Ordered Pairs

Name:_____

Date:_____

Reminder: The first number marks the distance across, and the second number indicates the vertical distance.

Nikki lost her ring during a trip to the park. She searched all of the places she had visited that afternoon. Use ordered pairs to follow Nikki as she looks for her ring.

1. She started at (1, 2). What was there?

_____

2. She went to (2, 3). What was there?

_____

3. She checked (2, 4). What was there?

_____

4. She rested at (3, 5). What was there?

_____

5. She looked carefully at (4, 5). What was there?

_____

6. She searched (5, 3). What was there?

_____

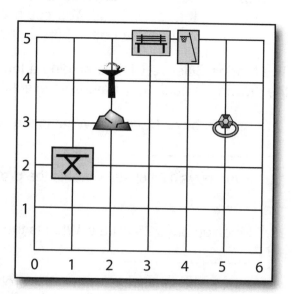

ACTIVITY 81 Tree Diagrams and Probability

Name:_____

Date:_____

Tree diagrams are a way to visualize possibilities. Use the information in the paragraph to label the diagram.

Casey has four shirts that are white, blue, tan, and yellow. She also has a pair of jeans, a pair of tan shorts, and a pair of denim shorts. How many outfits can she make? Fill in the tree diagram to find out.

_____

If she picks her shirt and pants at random, what is her probability of choosing a blue shirt and tan shorts? _____

ACTIVITY 82 Tree Diagrams and Probability

Name:_____

Date:_____

There is a toy vehicle giveaway this weekend at the local discount store. The shop owners are giving away toy cars, trucks, and vans. The vehicles are available in blue, red, green, silver, and copper. If all the toys are passed out at random, what is the probability of receiving a green truck?

_____

Draw a tree diagram and label it to demonstrate the solution. Draw a line for the toy cars, one for the trucks, and a third for the vans. On the left, draw linking lines to connect these limbs to the starting point. Add five branches at the right end of each line for the colors.

ACTIVITY 83   Measurement: Length— Inches, Feet, and Yards

Name:_____

Date:_____

Read about Jared's building project and answer the questions.

Jared is making a birdhouse. The wood pieces for the front and back of the house should each be $7\frac{1}{2}$″ long. The wood piece for each of the two sides should be 6″ long.

1. If Jared wants his dad to cut all of the sides from one board, how many inches long must that board be?_____

2. The lumberyard measures boards in feet and inches. There are 12 inches in a foot. How many feet and inches long must the board be?

    _____

3. The lumberyard sells boards only in 4′, 6′, and 8′ lengths. Which board should Jared buy? _____

4. How long, in feet and inches, will the leftover piece be?

    _____

ACTIVITY 84   Measurement: Length— Inches, Feet, and Yards

Name:_____

Date:_____

Read the information about Delia's project carefully, and then answer the questions.

Delia is taking a sewing class. Her first project is an apron. The waistband needs to be made from ribbon. To find out how much ribbon to buy, Delia will measure her waist and then add 18″ to each end for the two ties.

1. If Delia's waist measurement is 20″, how many inches long must her ribbon be?

    _____

2. The fabric store sells ribbon by the yard. If there are 36″ in a yard, how many yards of ribbon must Delia buy? _____

3. Delia finds some precut lengths of ribbon on sale. The ribbon comes in 1-, 2-, and 3-yard lengths. Which length will Delia buy? _____

4. How much ribbon will be left over? Write your answer in feet and inches. _____

ACTIVITY 85   Measurement: Length—
Up to a Meter

Name: _____

Date: _____

Centimeters and meters are metric measurements. Metric measurements are based on multiples of ten. There are 100 centimeters in one meter.

Gregory, Leo, and Nathan held a caterpillar race. They marked off the course in centimeters. The critter that traveled the farthest in three minutes would be the winner. When the race ended, the caterpillars had traveled the distances shown in the picture. (Note: All caterpillars were handled gently and released after the race.)

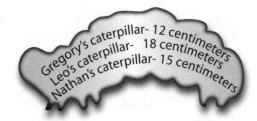

Gregory's caterpillar- 12 centimeters
Leo's caterpillar- 18 centimeters
Nathan's caterpillar- 15 centimeters

1. How far did the winning caterpillar travel? _____
2. How far did the losing caterpillar travel? _____
3. What was the total distance traveled by all of the caterpillars? _____
4. What was the average distance traveled by the caterpillars? _____
5. If all three caterpillars continue to travel at the same rate for five more minutes, would their total distance in that five minutes equal one meter? _____

ACTIVITY 86   Measurement: Length—
Up to a Meter

Name: _____

Date: _____

The diameter of a sphere is the length of a line segment passing through its center. A 2 cm sphere will have a diameter of 2 cm, no matter which way it is turned. Read the information, study the chart, and answer each question.

Bonnie	30 beads
Amanda	25 beads
Dawn	40 beads
Alicia	20 beads

Bonnie, Amanda, Dawn, and Alicia had a craft party on Saturday. The girls each made different amounts of beads out of craft clay, and then they each made a necklace with the finished beads. The diameter of each bead was 2 cm.

1. If the girls strung all of their beads together, how long would the finished string be?

_____

2. How long was Bonnie's string? _____
3. How long was the shortest string? _____
4. Whose finished string was exactly 0.5 m long? _____
5. What was the average length of the four strings? _____

ACTIVITY 87   Measurement: Length— Foot to Mile

Name:_____

Date:_____

Reminder: A mile is 5,280 feet.

Danny, Martin, Jack, and Steve took part in a charity run last weekend. Contributors pledged one cent for each foot of the course the boys completed.

Participants	Distance Run (in ft.)
Danny	5,280
Martin	7,920
Jack	9,240
Steve	10,560

1. There are three feet in a yard; how many yards did Danny run? _____

2. If Danny ran exactly a mile, how far did Steve run? _____

3. How many yards did Jack run? _____

4. How many more yards did Martin run than Danny? (Hint: Be careful! This involves two steps.) _____

Challenge: How much did all four boys earn for the charity? _____

ACTIVITY 88   Measurement: Length— Foot to Mile

Name:_____

Date:_____

Reminder: A mile is 5,280 feet.

Terry, Janet, Andrea, and Morgan took horseback riding lessons at camp last summer. Here are the distances each girl traveled during three days of lessons.

Riders	Distance Traveled (in ft.)
Terry	2,640
Janet	1,320
Andrea	3,960
Morgan	5,280

1. Which girl traveled exactly one mile? _____

2. Which girl traveled exactly $\frac{1}{2}$ mile? _____

3. How many yards did Andrea travel? _____

4. How many more feet did Morgan travel than Janet? _____

ACTIVITY 89 **Measurement: Length—**
Meter to Kilometer

Name:_____

Date:_____

In the metric system, the kilometer, or thousand meter measure, is used to mark greater distances.

In December of 2006, the Cassini spacecraft discovered a mountain range on Titan, the largest of Saturn's moons. The range is 150 km long, 30 km wide, and about 1.5 km high.

1. There are 1,000 meters in a kilometer. How many meters long is Titan's mountain range? _____

2. How many meters wide is the range? _____

3. About how many meters high are the mountains? _____

4. Mt. Everest is about 8,850 m tall. How much taller is Mt. Everest than the peaks in Titan's mountain range? _____

- -

ACTIVITY 90 **Measurement: Length—**
Meter to Kilometer

Name:_____

Date:_____

When writing out the height of each mountain, use the word "and" to stand for the decimal point.

Example: 1.2 = one and two tenths.

The World's Tallest Mountains

Mountain	Height (in m)
Mt. Everest	8,850
K2	8,611
Kanchenjunga	8,586
Lhotse	8,516
Makalu	8,463

1. K2 is 8.611 km tall; how tall is Mt. Everest in kilometers? Write out the height of Mt. Everest in words. _____

2. How many kilometers tall is Makalu? Write out the height of Makalu in words.

_____

3. According to this table, how much taller is Mt. Everest than K2? Write your answer in meters. _____

4. How much taller is Kanchenjunga than Lhotse? Write your answer in meters.

_____

ACTIVITY 91   Perimeter and Area

Name:_____

Date:_____

Perimeter is the distance around the outside of a shape. Area is the space that is contained within a shape. To find the perimeter of a rectangle, multiply the width by two and the length by two, and then add the results. To find the area of a rectangle, multiply the length by the width. Your answer will be in square units.

20'

16'

Becky is redecorating her room. She wants to buy a wallpaper border for the perimeter of her walls and carpet squares to cover the area of her floor. Her room is 16 ft. x 20 ft.

1. Each carpet square is 12 in. x 12 in. How many squares will Becky need for her room? _____

2. How many feet of the border will Becky need? _____

3. The border is measured in yards. How many yards will Becky need? _____

4. Becky wants to paint one of the long walls pale pink. To figure out how much paint to buy, Becky must know the area of the wall in square feet. If the wall is 8 feet tall and twenty feet long, what is its area in square feet? _____

20'

8'

ACTIVITY 92   Perimeter and Area

Name:_____

Date:_____

Reminder: Perimeter = (2 x length) + (2 x width)
area = length x width.

Mathematicians use these shorthand formulas: $P = 2l + 2w$ and $A = lw$.

Jacob and Sam are helping prepare the park for the annual summer chess tournament.

14 m

11 m

1. The boys need to fence off the perimeter of an area that is 11 m long and 14 m wide. How many meters of fencing do they need? _____

2. What is the size of the fenced-off tournament area in square meters? _____

3. Next, the boys make a sign to hang near the entrance of the tournament area. It is 1 m high and 2 m long. How many square meters of paper do they use for the sign? _____

4. They glue a strip of red ribbon along the outside edges of the sign. How many meters of ribbon do they use? _____

2 m

1 m

ACTIVITY 93   Volume

Name:_____

Date:_____

To find the volume of a solid, multiply the length times the width times the height, or $V = l \cdot w \cdot h$. Your answer will be in cubic units.

Ron's service club helped to pack boxes with donated supplies for schools damaged in a flood. Ron packed kindergarten building blocks into a box. Each block was 1 ft. long, 1 ft. tall, and 1 ft. wide. The box was 3 ft. long, 2 ft. tall, and 2 ft. wide.

1. What was the size, in cubic feet, of each block? _____

2. How many blocks could Ron pack into the box? _____

3. There were still more blocks to pack, so Ron found another box. It was 4 ft. long, 2 ft. tall, and 1 ft. deep. How many blocks could he pack into that box?

_____

4. After packing the second box, Ron still had 16 blocks left. Circle the box he should choose.

   A. a 2 ft. x 2 ft. x 2 ft. box   B. a 4 ft. x 4 ft. x 2 ft. box

   C. a 4 ft. x 2 ft. x 2 ft. box

ACTIVITY 94   Metric Volume

Name:_____

Date:_____

The superscripted ^{3} stands for cubic units.
For example, 3 m^3 means 3 cubic meters. Read the paragraph, and use the information to answer the questions. ***Reminder:*** $V = l \cdot w \cdot h$

Volunteers created a raised bed for a new garden at the botanical garden and planned to fill it with rich topsoil. The wooden bed they built was 40 cm deep, 85 cm long, and 90 cm wide.

1. How many cubic centimeters of topsoil would be needed to fill the container?

   _____

2. One cubic meter is 100 cm x 100 cm x 100 cm. How many cubic centimeters are there in one cubic meter? _____

3. If a farmer donated $\frac{1}{2}$ cubic meter (0.5 m^3) of clean topsoil, the volunteers would:

   A. have just enough soil.   B. have topsoil left over.   C. need more soil.

   Explain your answer. _____

4. The truck bed was 110 cm wide, 205 cm long, and 57 cm deep. How many cubic centimeters of soil could the farmer carry in one trip? _____

5. Would the farmer be able to deliver all of the soil at once, or would he need to make several trips? _____

ACTIVITY 95 Measurement: Weight— Ounces and Pounds

Name:_____

Date:_____

Ounces and pounds are common units of weight measurement used in America.

1. There are 16 ounces in a pound. Which balls weigh more than a pound? _____

2. A sports store ships 10 baseballs to a team's coach. How many ounces do the balls weigh? _____ How many pounds do they weigh? Write your answer as a mixed number. _____

Equipment	Approx. Weight
baseball	5 oz.
tennis ball	2 oz.
soccer ball	16 oz.
basketball	20 oz.

3. A sports team flew to a week-long training camp. They brought 5 balls with them. The balls weighed about 5 pounds. What kind of team was it? _____

4. Sweet Shot tennis balls come packed one pound per box. How many are there per box? _____

5. The gym coach bought a baseball, a tennis ball, a soccer ball, and a basketball. How much did his purchase weigh in ounces? _____ How much did it weigh in pounds? _____

ACTIVITY 96 Measurement: Weight— Ounces and Pounds

Name:_____

Date:_____

Answer these questions about the perfect apples from April Orchard.

Few apples are exactly the same size, but at April Orchard, each apple weighs exactly 4 ounces.

1. How many April Orchard apples are in a pound? _____

2. How many of these apples are in 5 pounds? _____

3. There a 2,000 pounds in a ton. How many April Orchard apples are in a ton? _____

4. If Jan had a pound of April Orchard apples and she ate one, how many ounces of apples would she have left? _____

ACTIVITY 97   Measurement: Weight—Grams and Kilograms

Name:_____

Date:_____

Grams and kilograms are units of weight measurement in the metric system. A kilogram is equal to a thousand grams. Answer these weighty questions about elephants in the wild.

In the wild, an adult African elephant eats between 100 and 200 kg of vegetation each day.

1. If an elephant eats 112 kg of long grass, how many grams of grass has he eaten? _____

2. If an elephant eats 8,000 grams of fruit, how many kilograms of fruit has he eaten? _____

3. If an elephant eats 12 kg of baobab tree twigs, how many grams of wood has he eaten? _____

4. If an elephant eats everything in number 1, number 2, and number 3, how many kilograms of plant material has he eaten? _____

ACTIVITY 98   Measurement: Weight—Kilograms and Metric Tons

Name:_____

Date:_____

Reminder: Add tags, such as km or g, to your answer.

The West Bay ferry can carry cars and trucks weighing a total of 236 metric tons.

Vehicle	Weight (in kg)
Car	1,200
Pickup	2,200
Van	2,800
Delivery truck	6,000

1. There are 1,000 kilograms in a metric ton. How many kilograms can the ferry safely carry? _____

2. What is the weight of 200 cars in kilograms? _____
   In metric tons? _____

3. What is the weight of 200 pickups in kilograms? _____
   In metric tons? _____

4. Can the ferry carry 200 cars? _____
   Can the ferry carry 100 cars and 50 pickups? _____

Challenge: What is the weight of one car, one pickup, one van, and one delivery truck in metric tons? _____

ACTIVITY 99 Elapsed Time

Name:_____

Date:_____

There are sixty minutes in an hour, thirty minutes in half an hour, and fifteen minutes in a quarter of an hour.

Tinsdale High is hosting a Drama Workshop. Sue is answering phone calls about the schedule. How long should she tell people the following events last?

1. Welcome Assembly _____
2. Break _____
3. Theater Games _____
4. Reader's Theater _____
5. What is the total amount of time scheduled for breaks? _____
6. What is the total amount of time workshop participants will spend doing Theater Games and Reader's Theater? _____

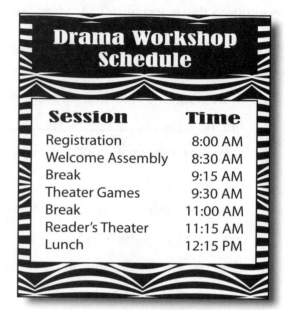

Drama Workshop Schedule

Session	Time
Registration	8:00 AM
Welcome Assembly	8:30 AM
Break	9:15 AM
Theater Games	9:30 AM
Break	11:00 AM
Reader's Theater	11:15 AM
Lunch	12:15 PM

ACTIVITY 100 Elapsed Time

Name:_____

Date:_____

Tommy is going to summer camp for the first time. He wants to study the schedule so he knows what to expect. Each event begins as soon as the last one ends.

1. How long must campers wait from the end of breakfast to the beginning of lunch?

   _____

2. How long does the hike last?

   _____

3. How long do campers have to shower and dress in the morning?

   _____

4. How long is the lunch period?

   _____

5. How long is the morning meeting?

   _____

Program for Camp Blue Lake:

Tuesday Schedule:

Event	Time
Wake Up	7:00 AM
Breakfast	8:20 AM
Morning Meeting	9:05 AM
Hike	9:30 AM
Free Time	11:00 AM
Lunch	12:25 PM
Crafts	1:00 PM
Swimming	2:30 PM

ACTIVITY 101   Speed and Distance

Name: _____

Date: _____

Since there are sixty minutes in an hour, a car that travels sixty miles per hour (mph) travels one mile every minute.

On a camping trip to High Mountain National Park, Mark's family follows this route.

1. At 60 mph, how long did it take Mark's family to get from home to Clear Lake? _____

2. Mark's father drives 60 mph without stopping. How many hours does it take to get from home to Evergreen Campground? _____

3. Mark's friend Danny lives in High Pass. How far is High Pass from Mark's home? _____

4. If Mark's family drove 60 mph and arrived at Danny's house at 4:00 P.M., when did they leave home?
_____

Place	Distance from Home
Clear Lake	60 miles
Ellentown Diner	95 miles
High Pass	120 miles
Evergreen Campgrounds	180 miles

ACTIVITY 102   Speed and Distance

Name: _____

Date: _____

Reminder: 1 km = 1,000 m

During his first charity cycle ride, Stuart pedaled at a rate of 6 kilometers per hour. The checkpoints on the course are shown on the diagram.

1. How long did it take Stuart to ride from the starting line to Lakeside Station?
_____

2. How long did it take Stuart to ride from Hilltop Station to Rose Garden Station?
_____

3. How long did it take Stuart to ride from the starting line to Hilltop Station? _____

4. How long did it take Stuart to ride the entire course?
_____

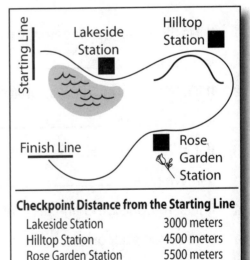

Checkpoint Distance from the Starting Line	
Lakeside Station	3000 meters
Hilltop Station	4500 meters
Rose Garden Station	5500 meters
Finish Line	6000 meters

ACTIVITY 103 Time Zones

Name:_____

Date:_____

Use the map to count time zones and find the differences in time across the continent.

Reminder: A.M. means between midnight and noon; P.M. means between noon and midnight. Subtract one hour for each time zone counted in a westerly direction.

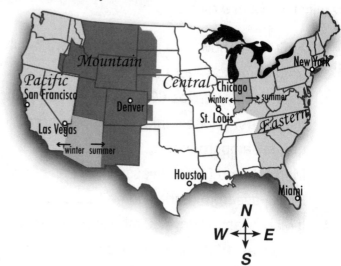

1. If it is 8:20 A.M. in San Francisco, what time is it in New York?

    _____

2. If it is 1:05 P.M. in Chicago, what time is it in Denver?

    _____

3. If it is 10:10 A.M. in St. Louis, what time is it in Las Vegas?

    _____

4. If it is 11:00 A.M. in Miami, what time is it in Houston? _____

- -

ACTIVITY 104 Time Zones

Name:_____

Date:_____

Use the map to count time zones and find the differences in time across the continent.
Reminder: A.M. means between midnight and noon; P.M. means between noon and midnight. Subtract one hour for each time zone counted in a westerly direction.

1. If it is 6:00 A.M. in Edmonton, what time is it in Halifax? _____

2. If it is 9:00 P.M. in Toronto, what time is it in Edmonton? _____

3. If it is 7:00 P.M. in Halifax, what time is it in Winnipeg? _____

4. If it is 10:00 A.M. in Winnipeg, what time is it in Vancouver?

    _____

ACTIVITY 105   Money

Name:_____

Date:_____

Check the facts, and then answer these questions about money. On your own paper, explain how you found the answers.

1. If ten dimes are equal to $1, how many dimes are equal to $5? _____

2. If ten nickels are equal to $\frac{1}{2}$ dollar, how many nickels are equal to $10? _____

3. If four quarters are equal to $1, how many quarters are equal to $20? _____

4. If ten pennies are equal to a dime, how many pennies are equal to 50 dimes? _____

5. Write three different combinations of three different coins that equal the value of a half dollar.

    _____, _____,

    _____

- -

ACTIVITY 106   Money

Name:_____

Date:_____

Check the facts, and then answer the questions about Canadian currency.

Canadian money has similar names and values to American money. The main difference is that Canada has a $1 coin, referred to as the "loonie," and a $2 coin, referred to as the "toonie."

0.01	0.05	0.10	0.25	1.00	2.00	5.00
penny	nickel	dime	quarter	dollar "loonie"	two dollars "toonie"	five dollar banknote

1. 200 pennies are equal to a toonie, and ten pennies are equal to a dime. How many dimes are equal to a toonie? _____

2. 25 pennies are equal to a quarter, and 100 pennies are equal to a loonie. How many quarters are equal to a $5 banknote? _____

3. Two loonies are equal to one toonie. 40 nickels are equal to one toonie. How many nickels are equal to one loonie? _____

4. Write three different combinations of coins that equal one toonie.

    _____, _____, _____

ACTIVITY 107 Money: Estimation

Name:_____

Date:_____

Estimation is an important skill. It helps when you are shopping. To estimate cash totals quickly, round off to the nearest dollar.

Jackie and Pat went to the store to buy supplies for the class party. Jackie filled the cart and Pat estimated the total to the nearest dollar as they shopped. The girls had $20 to spend.

Item	Price
1 bag of paper cups	0.83
1 package of napkins	0.59
1 carton of lemonade	2.29
1 bag of soy chips	2.32
1 container of dip	0.99

1. First, Jackie got two containers of dip and two bags of soy chips. Pat estimated those items cost: _____

2. Next, Jackie picked up two bags of cups and a package of napkins. Pat estimated those items cost: _____
   Pat then figured the estimated total value of all items in the basket as: _____

3. Finally, Jackie put four cartons of lemonade in the basket. Pat estimated the total cost of the lemonade at: _____

4. What was the exact value of the items in the basket? _____

5. How much different from the estimate was the actual total? _____

6. Did the girls have enough money to pay for everything? _____

ACTIVITY 108 Money: Estimation

Name:_____

Date:_____

Rounding off to the nearest dollar makes mental addition much easier.

Pete and Andrew went to the store to purchase supplies for a camping trip. Each had $20 to spend.

Item	Price
Flashlight	3.99
Lip balm	0.99
Insect repellent	2.68
Sunscreen	4.98

1. What was Pete's estimated total, to the nearest dollar, after he selected a flashlight and sunscreen?

   _____

2. What was Andrew's estimated total, to the nearest dollar, after he selected insect repellent and sunscreen? _____

3. How much, rounded to the nearest dollar, did each boy have left to spend?
   Pete: _____   Andrew: _____

4. What was each boy's actual total?
   Pete: _____   Andrew: _____

ACTIVITY 109 Money: Adding and Subtracting

Name: _____

Date: _____

When adding or subtracting money, keep the decimal points lined up. Remember to add the dollar signs.

Larry's service club collected money for children's cancer research. The fund-raising drive lasted for one week.

1. How much more money was raised on Tuesday than on Friday? _____

2. How much less money was raised on Wednesday than on Thursday? _____

3. How much money was raised on Monday and Tuesday? _____

4. How much money was raised during the entire week? _____

5. A business owner pledged to match the amount the service club raised. What was the total amount the club delivered to the charity?

   _____

Ledger	
MONEY COLLECTED	DOLLARS
Monday	$ 215.26
Tuesday	$ 309.20
Wednesday	$ 199.89
Thursday	$ 202.94
Friday	$ 103.47

ACTIVITY 110 Money: Adding and Subtracting

Name: _____

Date: _____

Decide whether to add or subtract.

For her geography report, Mandy planned a virtual trip to Italy.

1. How much did Mandy plan to spend on airfare and hotels? _____

2. How much did Mandy plan to spend on restaurants and entrance fees? _____

3. In all, how much did Mandy budget for her trip to Italy? _____

4. If her assignment allowed $1,700 for trip expenses, how much would Mandy have left for spending money? _____

Expense	Cost
AIRFARE	$615.28
HOTELS	$511.92
RESTAURANTS	$299.56
ENTRANCE FEES	$ 48.32
BUSES AND CABS	$107.12

ACTIVITY 111 Money: Multiplying

Name: _____

Date: _____

Reminder: When multiplying, do not forget the dollar signs and decimal points.

At the Cinco de Mayo festival, Midvale Middle School sold Mexican-inspired snacks to raise money for a summer camp scholarship.

1. How much did 5 tacos cost? _____

2. How much did 3 orders of nachos cost?

    _____

3. How much did 12 quesadillas cost?

    _____

4. How much did 15 sodas cost?

    _____

MENU

Item Sold:	Price per Item:
Taco	.89
Nachos	1.99
Quesadilla	.95
Soda	.85

ACTIVITY 112 Money: Multiplying

Name: _____

Date: _____

Reminder: Do not forget the dollar signs and decimal points.

Jenny bought supplies for an after-school art class.

1. How much did three pads of paper cost?

    _____

2. How much did 18 tubes of paint cost?

    _____

3. How much were 5 brushes? _____

4. How much were 12 pencils? _____

5. The shop was selling a prepackaged set of 12 pencils for $15.00. The set included a box that sold separately for $2.00. Was it a good buy? _____ Why or why not? _____

6. At the end of the session, the class had a show. Jenny sold a drawing for $100. After expenses, how much did she earn? _____

Item	Price per Item
pad of paper	4.67
tube of paint	2.99
brush	3.25
drawing pencil	1.05

ACTIVITY 113   Money: Dividing

Name:_____

Date:_____

When dividing money, watch the decimal places.
The decimal point in your quotient will be directly above the decimal point in your dividend. With cash, portions of a dollar are always written in hundredths. Example: $0.50

Felicia's mom took Felicia, Leslie, and Melissa to the amusement park, where she charged everything to her credit card. The girls agreed to split the expenses evenly to repay Felicia's mom.

1. How much did each girl owe for admission?

   _____

2. How much did each girl owe for snacks?

   _____

3. How much did each girl owe for photographs?

   _____

4. How much did each girl owe in all?

   _____

ABA ACE BANK OF ADA CREDIT ACCOUNT	
PURCHASE	AMOUNT
AMUSEMENT WORLD	
ADMISSION	$105.60
SNACKS	$ 15.75
LUNCH	$ 19.77
PHOTOGRAPHS	$ 8.97
SOUVENIRS	$ 18.45

ACTIVITY 114   Money: Dividing

Name:_____

Date:_____

Read the paragraph, and divide to answer these questions about a summer business partnership.

Christopher, Drew, Evan, Andres, and Benji formed a summertime yard care company. They agreed to work together on each project and to split their earnings equally. In the first week, they weeded Mrs. Cody's yard and earned $20.25. Next, they mowed Mr. Brian's yard and earned $6.50. They earned $5.20 for raking the leaves in Ms. Carson's yard, and $2.50 for sweeping Mrs. Amira's walkway. Finally, they planted Mr. Courtney's tomatoes, and he paid them $12.45.

1. How much did each boy earn for pulling Mrs. Cody's weeds? _____

2. How much did each boy earn for planting Mr. Courtney's tomatoes?

   _____

3. How much did each boy earn for mowing Mr. Brian's lawn? _____

4. How much did each boy earn for his first week's work? _____

5. If each boy collected $137.40 for 12 weeks of work, how much did he earn per week?

   _____

   If each boy worked 5 hours per week, how much did he earn per hour? _____

ACTIVITY 115   Basic Operations With Numbers More Than 1,000

Name:_____

Date:_____

Large numbers take longer to add, subtract, multiply, and divide, but the operations and the basic facts are the same. For accurate results, work neatly. Adding tens to hundreds because of a crooked column of numbers wastes your time.

1. The largest cave chamber in the world is Sarawak Chamber in Malaysia. It is 2,300 ft. long, 980 ft. wide, and 230 ft. high. What is the volume of the chamber in cubic feet?
    _____

2. Mammoth Cave in Kentucky, USA, is the longest cave system in the world. It is 348 miles long. If there are 5,280 feet in a mile, how many feet long is the system?
    _____

3. The Lukina Jama Cave in Croatia is 4,566 ft. deep. Réseau Jean Bernard Cave in France is 5,036 ft. deep. Krubera in the western Caucasus region of Georgia, is at least 6,824 ft. deep. According to these numbers, how much deeper is Krubera than Réseau Jean Bernard? _____

4. How much deeper is Krubera than Lukina Jama? _____

ACTIVITY 116   Basic Operations With Numbers More Than 1,000

Name:_____

Date:_____

After deciding which operation to use, check your work carefully.

1. What is the average area, in square kilometers, of the world's four largest seas?
    _____

2. What is the average depth, in meters, of the world's four largest seas? _____

3. Which sea is about $\frac{1}{2}$ as deep as the Caribbean Sea? _____

4. How much deeper is the Caribbean Sea than the Mediterranean Sea? _____

The World's Four Largest Seas		
Name	Depth in Meters	Area in Square Kilometers
South China Sea	1,200	2,974,600
Caribbean Sea	2,400	2,753,000
Mediterranean Sea	1,485	2,503,800
Bering Sea	1,400	2,268,180

ACTIVITY 117 Three-Digit Divisors

Name: _____

Date: _____

When working with three-digit divisors, you will need to estimate, and then use trial and error.

Answer these questions about the Monroe City recycling drive.

1. 375 students at Lane Avenue School collected 47,250 plastic grocery bags for recycling. If all students brought in the same number of bags, how many bags did each one collect?

   _____

2. 432 students at Parker Road School collected 57,024 bags. If all students brought in the same number of bags, how many did each one collect? _____

3. At Davis Street School, 274 students brought in 54,526 bags. If all students brought in the same number of bags, how many did each one collect? _____

4. At which school did each student bring in the most bags? _____

ACTIVITY 118 Three-Digit Divisors

Name: _____

Date: _____

Divide to answer the questions.

1. If there are 6,945 library books for 463 students at Martin Lane School, how many books are there per student?

   _____

2. If there are 1,490 textbooks for 298 students at Lacey Street School, how many textbooks are there per student?

   _____

3. If 307 students at Table Mountain School use 7,675 sheets of paper per week, and all students use the same amount of paper, how many sheets does each student use?

   _____

4. If 299 students at Oceanside School spend a total of $7,678.32 on school supplies, and all students spend the same amount, how much does each student spend?

   _____

ACTIVITY 119 Range, Median, and Mean

Name:_____

Date:_____

The **range** is the difference between the highest and lowest numbers in a group. The **median** is the number in the middle of the group of numbers when the numbers are arranged in order. If there are two numbers in the middle, the median is the average of those two numbers. The **mean** is the average of all of the numbers in a group.

Dustin took a poll to find out where students wanted to go on a school-sponsored trip.

1. What is the mean? _____
2. What is the median? _____
3. What is the range? _____
4. How many students responded to this poll?

   _____
5. There are 956 students at the school. How many did not respond? _____

Challenge: If you were a local business owner thinking about sponsoring a trip, how would this poll help you?

_____

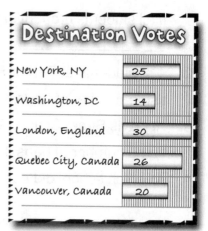

Destination Votes

New York, NY	25
Washington, DC	14
London, England	30
Quebec City, Canada	26
Vancouver, Canada	20

ACTIVITY 120 Range, Median, and Mean

Name:_____

Date:_____

The **range** is the difference between the highest and lowest numbers in a group. The **median** is the number in the middle of a group of numbers when the numbers are arranged in order. If there are two numbers in the middle, the median is the average of those two numbers. The **mean** is the average of all of the numbers in a group.

Delinda took a poll on her blog to find out which television shows her readers were watching on Saturday nights.

1. What is the mean? _____
2. Which shows have scores above the mean?

   _____

   _____
3. What is the median? _____ Which show has the median score? _____
4. What is the range? _____ What does this tell you about the five shows? _____
5. How many people participated in the poll? _____

Challenge: How could advertisers use this information? Answer on your own paper.

Show	Number of Watchers
The Big Littles	254
Mark Anders, Middle School Detective	1,351
Talent Incorporated	2,194
From the Director's Chair	187
Dear Andrea	316

ACTIVITY 121   Adding and Subtracting Unlike Fractions

Name:_____

Date:_____

Before adding or subtracting unlike fractions, you must change them to like fractions.

Jan's mom cut up four apples. She cut apple A in half and apple B into fourths. She cut apple C into sixths and apple D into eighths.

1. If Jan took one piece of apple A and one piece of apple B, what fraction of a whole apple would she have? _____

2. If Jan took one piece of apple B and one piece of apple D, what fraction of a whole apple would she have? _____

3. If Jan took one piece of apple A and two pieces of apple C, what fraction of a whole apple would she have? _____

4. If Jan took one piece of apple A and one piece of apple D, what fraction of a whole apple would she have? _____

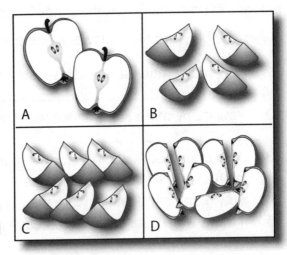

ACTIVITY 122   Adding and Subtracting Unlike Fractions

Name:_____

Date:_____

For Jake's first carpentry project, his dad helped him cut up four identical boards. He cut board A into thirds and board B into sixths. He cut board C into ninths and board D into twelfths. Divide the four boards as indicated and label each one. Then, answer the questions below.

1. If Jake selected one piece of board A and one piece of board D, what fraction of a whole board would he have? _____

2. List at least two ways Jake could make $\frac{1}{2}$ of a board. _____,

   _____

3. List at least two ways Jake could make $\frac{1}{3}$ of a whole board. _____,

   _____

4. What could Jake add to four pieces of board D and three pieces of board C to equal the length of a whole board? _____

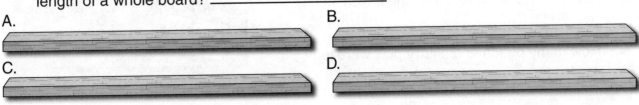

A.

B.

C.

D.

61

ACTIVITY 123 **Adding and Subtracting Mixed Numbers**

Name:_____

Date:_____

At 1:00 P.M. there were three plates on the picnic table. Plate A had $3\frac{1}{2}$ peanut butter sandwiches. Plate B had $2\frac{3}{4}$ cheese sandwiches, and Plate C had $2\frac{3}{8}$ bologna sandwiches. Draw the sandwiches on the plates at right, and then answer these questions.

1. How many more sandwiches were on Plate A than on Plate B? _____
2. How many more sandwiches were on Plate A than on Plate C? _____
3. Brad does not like bologna. How many sandwiches did he have to choose from? _____
4. How many sandwiches were there in all? _____
5. If there were 5 sandwiches on each plate at the start of the picnic, how many had been eaten? _____

ACTIVITY 124 **Adding and Subtracting Mixed Numbers**

Name:_____

Date:_____

When Sue visited the school fair at 3:00 P.M., three tables displayed pies for sale. On table A, there were $4\frac{1}{3}$ apple pies. On table B, there were $2\frac{5}{6}$ peach pies, and on table C, there were $1\frac{1}{12}$ cherry pies. Answer these questions about the pies.

1. If there were 10 apple pies at the beginning of the fair, how many were sold before Sue arrived?

   _____

2. How many more apple pies were left than cherry pies? _____

3. How many pies were left on the tables, in all?

   _____

4. How many peach and cherry pies were left?

   _____

ACTIVITY 125 **Multiplying Mixed Numbers: Area**

Name:_____

Date:_____

Before multiplying mixed numbers, change them to improper fractions. After multiplying, change them back to mixed numbers.

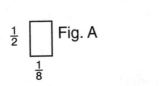

$\frac{1}{2}$ ☐ Fig. A
$\frac{1}{8}$

$2\frac{1}{2}$ Fig. B
$1\frac{3}{4}$

1. The sides of figure B measure $2\frac{1}{2}$ ft. x $1\frac{3}{4}$ ft. Find the perimeter. _____

2. Find the area of figure B. _____

3. The sides of figure A measure $\frac{1}{2}$ ft. x $\frac{1}{8}$ ft. Find the perimeter. _____

4. Find the area of figure A. _____

5. If figure A were attached to one side of figure B, what would the area of the new figure be?
_____

ACTIVITY 126 **Multiplying Mixed Numbers: Area**

Name:_____

Date:_____

Before multiplying mixed numbers, change them to improper fractions. After multiplying, change them back to mixed numbers.

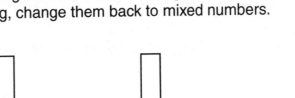

Arthur's Room Arthur's Bathroom Arthur's Closet

1. Arthur's room is $14\frac{1}{2}$ ft. x $10\frac{1}{4}$ ft. Label the diagram. Find the perimeter. _____

2. Find the area of Arthur's room. _____

3. Arthur's bathroom is $6\frac{1}{4}$ ft. x $5\frac{1}{2}$ ft. Label the diagram. Find the area. _____

4. Arthur's closet is $2\frac{1}{4}$ ft. x $6\frac{1}{4}$ ft. Label the diagram. Find the area. _____

5. What is the total area of Arthur's room, bathroom, and closet? _____

ACTIVITY 127 Dividing Fractions

Name:_____

Date:_____

To divide fractions, use the reciprocal of the divisor to multiply the dividend.

Example: $\frac{3}{4} \div \frac{2}{3} = \frac{3}{4} \times \frac{3}{2}$. Read the problems and answer the questions.

Jake and his family share a new computer. Friday night is Jake's turn. He has $1\frac{1}{4}$ hours after dinner to use the machine.

1. On his first Friday night, Jake sent e-mails to his friends. If each e-mail took $\frac{1}{8}$ of an hour to finish, how many e-mails did he send? _____

2. On his second Friday night, Jake played his favorite computer game. If each level took $\frac{1}{2}$ of an hour to finish, how many levels did he complete? _____

3. On his third Friday night, Jake wrote movie reviews in his blog. If each review took $\frac{1}{3}$ of an hour to finish, how many reviews did he write? _____

4. On his fourth Friday night, Jake chatted with friends. If he chatted with each friend for $\frac{1}{4}$ of an hour, how many friends did he contact? _____

ACTIVITY 128 Dividing Fractions

Name:_____

Date:_____

To divide fractions, use the reciprocal of the divisor to multiply the dividend.

Example: $\frac{3}{4} \div \frac{2}{3} = \frac{3}{4} \times \frac{3}{2}$. Read the problems and answer the questions.

Mrs. Wilson, the art teacher, had a $6\frac{1}{2}$ square foot (sq. ft.) sheet of white paper.

1. She needed squares that were $\frac{3}{4}$ of a sq. ft. for a project. How many $\frac{3}{4}$ ft. squares could she cut from the $6\frac{1}{2}$ sq. ft. sheet of paper? _____

2. She decided to make the squares a little smaller. How many $\frac{1}{2}$ ft. squares could she cut from the $6\frac{1}{2}$ sq. ft. sheet? _____

3. Mr. Davis gave Mrs. Wilson a larger sheet of pale blue paper. It was $7\frac{3}{8}$ sq. ft. How many $\frac{1}{2}$ ft. squares could she cut from the blue paper? _____

4. Since she had more paper, Mrs. Wilson decided to make each square slightly larger. How many $\frac{5}{8}$ ft. squares could she cut from the $7\frac{3}{8}$ sq. ft. paper? _____

ACTIVITY 129 Multiplying With Decimal Fraction Multipliers

Name: _____

Date: _____

To multiply a whole number by a decimal fraction, simply multiply as usual. The decimal must be in the same place in the product as it is in the multiplier.

Example:
```
   12
x 0.2
-----
  2.4
```

Students at Pleasant Valley Middle School

Grade	# of Students
6	170
7	140
8	160

1. Nine-tenths of the students in the seventh grade will be returning to Pleasant Valley Middle School next year. How many seventh-graders will be returning? _____ How many will not be returning? _____

2. Five-hundredths of the students in the eighth grade will be attending an honors high school program. How many of the eighth-graders will be part of the program? _____

3. Two-tenths of the students in the sixth grade will sign up for the school service club. How many sixth graders will sign up? _____

4. Three-tenths of the seventh-graders are already in the club. How many seventh-graders are in the school service club? _____

ACTIVITY 130 Multiplying With Decimal Fraction Multipliers

Name: _____

Date: _____

Example:
```
   12
x 0.2
-----
  2.4
```

To multiply a whole number by a decimal fraction, simply multiply as usual. The decimal must be in the same place in the product as it is in the multiplier.

1. Five-hundredths of the money raised in 2005 was used for postage. How much was spent on postage? _____

2. Three-thousandths of the money raised in 2006 was used to buy lightbulbs for the office. How much was spent on lightbulbs? _____

3. Six-tenths of the money raised in 2007 was used to support the food bank. How much money was used to support the food bank? _____

4. Four-tenths of the money raised in 2008 was used to support the Clothing Exchange Shop. How much money was used to support the Clothing Exchange Shop?

_____

MONEY RAISED FOR COMMUNITY HOPE

YEAR	DOLLARS
2005	$3,295
2006	$4,255
2007	$2,600
2008	$3,540

ACTIVITY 131 Dividing With Decimal Fraction Divisors

Name:_____

Date:_____

Before dividing by a decimal fraction, you can multiply both the divisor and the dividend by ten, one hundred, or one thousand to eliminate the decimal point in the divisor.

Example: $9.3 \div 3.1$ $9.3 \times 10 = 93$ $3.1 \times 10 = 31$ $93 \div 31 = 3$

$$3.1 \overline{)9.3}$$

Divide to answer the questions. Round decimal fractions to the nearest hundredth if necessary.

Cynthia had 6.5 liters of lemonade.

1. How many 0.25-liter cups of lemonade could she fill?

    _____

2. How many 1.8-liter pitchers could she fill? _____

3. How many 0.95-liter hiker's bottles could she fill? _____

4. How many 0.35-liter glasses could she fill? _____

ACTIVITY 132 Dividing With Decimal Fraction Divisors

Name:_____

Date:_____

Before dividing by a decimal fraction, you can multiply both the divisor and the dividend by ten, one hundred, or one thousand to eliminate the decimal point in the divisor. Divide to answer the questions. Round decimal fractions to the nearest hundredth if necessary.

Regina's mother is a cancer survivor, so Regina is raising money for cancer research. A sewing shop donated 5.05 meters of pink ribbon.

1. Pink bow pins for the cancer awareness campaign take 0.20 meters of ribbon each. How many pink bows could Regina make with the ribbon?

    _____

2. Wrapping gifts for cancer patients in the hospital takes 0.82 meters of ribbon per gift. How many gifts could Regina wrap? _____

3. Making necklaces for the group's gift shop takes 0.65 meters of ribbon per necklace. How many necklaces could Regina make? _____

4. Pink ribbon refrigerator door magnets take 0.05 meters of ribbon per magnet. How many magnets could Regina decorate? _____

Daily Skill Builders: Word Problems

ACTIVITY 133   Percents

Name: _____

Date: _____

Percent means portion of a hundred. To find the
percentage, divide the target number by the total possible.

Example: 10 out of 100 is $\frac{10}{100}$, which is the same as 0.10, or 10%.

Round the answer to the nearest percent.

On the first history test of the year, Victor got only 20 out of 50 questions correct. On the second test, Victor studied hard and got 10 out of 10 questions correct. For the third test, Victor didn't study as hard, and got 75 out of 90 questions right. Victor studied more for the fourth test and wound up getting 25 correct out of 30.

1. What percentage of correct answers did Victor score on the first test? _____

2. What was Victor's percentage of correct answers on the second test? _____

3. What percentage of correct answers did Victor score on the third test? _____

4. What was Victor's percentage of correct answers on the fourth test? _____

5. What was the average percentage of Victor's history test scores? _____

6. If 90% and above was an A, 80% and above was a B, and 70% and above was a C, what was Victor's history grade? _____

ACTIVITY 134   Percents

Name: _____

Date: _____

Percent means portion of a hundred. To find the
percentage, divide the target number by the total possible.

Example: 10 out of 100 is $\frac{10}{100}$, which is the same as 0.10, or 10%.

Round the answers to the nearest percent.

1. What percentage of baskets did Ken score in August? _____

2. What percentage of baskets did Javier score in August? _____

3. What percentage of baskets did Graham score in August? _____

4. What percentage of baskets did Leo score in August? _____

5. Which player sank the greatest percentage of baskets in August? _____

Basketball Practice August

	Baskets	Shots
Ken	40	152
Javier	83	194
Graham	76	99
Leo	92	105

ACTIVITY 135 Ratios

Name:_____

Date:_____

Ratios compare numbers. They are written in this form: 12:2.

The West Valley Botanical Gardens has a beautiful rose garden. There are 25 red roses, 50 pink roses, 15 yellow roses, and only 10 white roses.

1. The ratio of red roses to pink roses is 25: _____, 50: _____, or

    100: _____.

2. The ratio of white to yellow roses is _____ :15, 20: _____, or 30:

    _____.

3. The ratio of pink roses to white roses is 50: _____, 5: _____, or

    100: _____.

4. The ratio of yellow roses to red roses is 15: _____, 30: _____, or

    _____ :100.

ACTIVITY 136 Ratios

Name:_____

Date:_____

Ratios compare numbers. They are written in this form: 12:2.

Cherish inherited her grandmother's button box. Here are the types of buttons she found in the box. Inside, there were 30 glass buttons, 60 buttons made from shells, 100 plastic buttons, and 40 wooden buttons.

1. The ratio of wooden buttons to plastic buttons is 40: _____, 2: _____, or
    4: _____.

2. The ratio of wooden buttons to shell buttons is 40: _____, 2: _____, or
    4: _____.

3. The ratio of glass buttons to plastic buttons is 30: _____, 3: _____, or
    6: _____.

4. The ratio of shell buttons to plastic buttons is 60: _____, 6: _____, or
    _____ :20.

ACTIVITY 137 Proportions

Name: _____

Date: _____

A ratio can also be written as a fraction. To find an unknown number in a pair of ratios, cross-multiply. For example, $\frac{2}{3} = \frac{?}{6}$. The missing number is 4 because $2 \times 6 = 12$ and $3 \times 4 = 12$.

Jake constructs scale model buildings for the town museum. He measures the Old Town Hall carefully to make his model as accurate as possible. Jake uses two centimeters to represent each meter in his model.

1. How long will each of the miniature town hall's sides be? 2 cm/1 m = _____ cm/20 m

2. How wide will the model building be?
   2 cm/1 m = _____ cm/15 m

3. How wide will the model's front door be?
   2 cm/1 m = _____ cm/2 m

4. How tall will the model's front door be?
   2 cm/1 m = _____ cm/3 m

Measurements of the Old Town Hall

Building Part	Measurement in Meters
Length of each side	20
Length of front and back	15
Width of front door	2
Height of front door	3

ACTIVITY 138 Proportions

Name: _____

Date: _____

A ratio can also be written as a fraction.

To find an unknown number in a pair of ratios, cross-multiply. For example, $\frac{2}{3} = \frac{?}{6}$. The missing number is 4 because $2 \times 6 = 12$ and $3 \times 4 = 12$.

Anna and Christina are preparing refreshments for a summer pool party.

1. For every measuring cup of punch mix, they are directed to use 6 measuring cups of water. Each measuring cup is about one serving, and the girls want to make 42 servings.

   How many cups of punch mix should they use? $\frac{1}{6} = \frac{}{42}$

For each two pizza snacks, they will need 1 English muffin, 2 oz. canned pizza sauce, two slices of cheese, and six slices of pepperoni.

2. How many English muffins will they need if they want to make 20 pizza snacks?

   $\frac{1}{2} = \frac{}{20}$

3. How many ounces of canned pizza sauce will they need? $\frac{2}{2} = \frac{}{20}$

4. How many slices of pepperoni will they need? $\frac{6}{2} = \frac{}{20}$

ACTIVITY 139   Three-Dimensional Forms

Name:_____

Date:_____

In a world with only two dimensions, how would three-dimensional objects appear?

In Flatworld, there are only two dimensions.

1. When lying down, this Flatworld character looks like either a point floating in space or a circle, but, when standing, he looks like a triangle. In our world, what three-dimensional shape would he be? _____

2. When lying down, this Flatworld character looks like a square. Actually, when seen from any of his six faces, this fellow looks exactly the same. In our world, what three-dimensional shape would he be? _____

3. When lying down, this Flatworld character looks like either a square or a point floating in space, but, when standing, he looks like a triangle. In our world, what three-dimensional shape would he be? _____

4. From any angle, this Flatworld character looks like a circle. In our world, what three-dimensional shape would he be? _____

5. What would a cylinder look like in Flatworld? Why? _____

ACTIVITY 140   Three-Dimensional Forms

Name:_____

Date:_____

Dimensional Detective Work

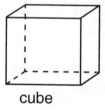
cube

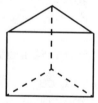
square pyramid

triangular prism

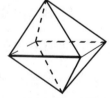
octahedron

1. I have 12 edges, 8 vertices, and all 6 of my faces are congruent.
    What am I? _____

2. I have 8 edges, 5 vertices, and only one of my 5 faces is square.
    What am I? _____

3. I have 12 edges, 6 vertices, and all of my eight faces are triangular.
    What am I? _____

4. I have 9 edges and 6 vertices. I also have five faces. Three of them are quadrilaterals, and two are triangles. What am I? _____

ACTIVITY 141 **Circumference**

Name:_____

Date:_____

Find the circumference of a circle by multiplying the radius by 2 and then multiplying the result by pi (π). For this exercise, round π off to the nearest hundredth (3.14).

Denise is making some signs for the spring dance. The theme is "Bubbles." She wants to glue heavy black yarn around the edges of different sizes of cardboard circles, but she needs to know how much yarn to buy.

1. The red circle has a radius of 30 cm. How much yarn does Denise need for the circumference? _____
2. The yellow circle has a radius of 20 cm. How much yarn does Denise need for the circumference? _____
3. The green circle has a radius of 45 cm. How much yarn does Denise need for the circumference? _____
4. The blue circle has a radius of 40 cm. How much yarn does Denise need for the circumference? _____
5. How much yarn does she need in all? _____

ACTIVITY 142 **Circumference**

Name:_____

Date:_____

Find the circumference of a circle by multiplying the radius by 2 and then multiplying the result by pi (π). For this exercise, round π off to the nearest hundredth (3.14).

Mark is helping his uncle build a fence around the exercise ring at his horse ranch.

1. The outer ring has a radius of 25 meters. How many meters of fencing will they need? _____
2. The inner ring will also need a special, lower fence. It has a radius of 6 meters. How much of the lower fencing will they need? _____
3. After they finish building the fences, Mark and his uncle will place circles of wire fencing around the bases of some young apple trees to protect their bark from grazing deer. The circle of wire around each trunk will have a radius of 25 cm. How much wire fencing will they need for each tree? _____

Challenge: If Mark stands in the ring holding a rope, and a tethered horse trots around him in a circle with a circumference of 18.84 m, how long is the rope? _____

ACTIVITY 143 Areas of Triangles

Name:_____

Date:_____

To find the area of a triangle, multiply $\frac{1}{2}$ times the base times the height, or $A = \frac{1}{2} bh$. Read the paragraph, and then answer the questions.

Jackie and Ellen want to have a large triangle painted on the wall of the recreation center. They need to know the number of square feet there will be in the triangle so they can order the correct amount of paint.

1. If the triangle has a base of 12 ft. and a height of 10 ft., how many square feet will it cover?

    _____

2. If the triangle has a base of 16 ft. and a height of 12 ft., how many square feet will it cover?

    _____

3. If the triangle has a base of 10 ft. and a height of 6 ft., how many square feet will it cover?

    _____

4. If the triangle has a base of 20 ft. and a height of 16 ft., how many square feet will it cover?

    _____

ACTIVITY 144 Areas of Complex Shapes

Name:_____

Date:_____

To find the area of a complex shape, find the area of each section, and then total the areas of the sections.

The floor plan for the botanical garden's new birdwatching shelter is made up of three parts. The main shelter is 12 ft. x 6 ft. The height of the triangular section is 4 ft. A small rectangular entryway is 6 ft. x 3 ft. Label each part of the drawing, and then answer the questions.

1. What is the area of the main shelter?

    _____

2. What is the area of the triangular section?

    _____

3. What is the area of the entryway?

    _____

4. What is the area of the entire shelter?

    _____

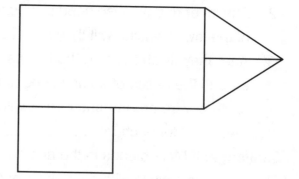

ACTIVITY 145 Pictographs

Name: _____

Date: _____

In a pictograph, each picture stands for a certain amount. Study the chart and answer the questions.

Jana surveyed the insects in her yard. In the pictograph, each insect represents 7 insects she counted.

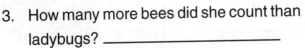

1. How many ants did she count?

   _____

2. How many more flies did she count than ladybugs?

   _____

3. How many more bees did she count than ladybugs? _____

4. How many insects did Jana count? _____

5. What was the ratio of ants to flies? _____

6. What was the proportion of ladybugs to flies? _____ /5 = 28/ _____

ACTIVITY 146 Pictographs

Name: _____

Date: _____

In a pictograph, each picture stands for a certain amount. Study the chart and answer the questions.

At the end of the school year, Mrs. Kramer took inventory of her desk. Each symbol represents 15 items.

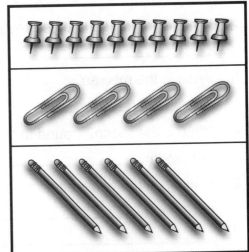

1. How many paper clips were in Mrs. Kramer's desk?

   _____

2. How many tacks were in Mrs. Kramer's desk?

   _____

3. How many more pencils than paper clips were there? _____

4. What was the ratio of tacks to paper clips?

   _____

5. How many items were in Mrs. Kramer's desk?

   _____

ACTIVITY 147 Surveys

Name:_____

Date:_____

Nicolas and Gabe surveyed their class on Monday to find out what everyone did on Saturday afternoons. They found that seven students participated in team sports, while six students worked on individual sports. Four students were involved with family activities, while five students checked "Other" on the survey.

1. How many students responded to the survey? _____

2. What is the range of these results? _____

3. What is the median? _____

4. What is the mean? _____

5. What is the ratio of students who played team sports to players of individual sports? _____

6. The proportion of participants in one of the activities compared to another activity is $\frac{3}{2}$. What are the activities?

_____   _____

ACTIVITY 148 Surveys

Name:_____

Date:_____

An election was coming up soon, so the *Hadleyville Times* polled its readers.

1. How many readers responded to the survey?

_____

2. What is the range of these results?

_____

3. What is the median?

_____

4. What is the mean? (round to the nearest hundredth) _____

5. Is this poll the same as an election? Why or why not? _____

_____

_____

HADLEYVILLE TIMES

Morning Edition   Local News   Tuesday

CANDIDATES GEARING UP FOR UPCOMING ELECTION.

LATEST POLL RESULTS:

CANDIDATE FOR MAYOR	NUMBER OF CHOICES
David Martinson	5,351
Javier Rodriguez	8,462
Tyrone Graham	8,520

ACTIVITY 149 Coordinate Graphing

Name:_____

Date:_____

In an ordered pair, the first number tells how many points to move horizontally on the grid and the second number tells how many points to move vertically.

A coded message arrived at headquarters. It is the missing character in a password. Decode the message by marking the location of each ordered pair on the grid.

1. Place a dot at (4, 4). Place a dot at (-4, -4). Draw a line connecting those two dots

2. Place a dot at (-4, 4) and a dot at (4, -4). Draw a line connecting those two dots.

What is the missing character? _____

Challenge: On your own grid, draw a polygon, and place points at each of the vertices. Describe the position of each of the points with an ordered pair. Write directions to solve, and invite a partner to recreate your polygon.

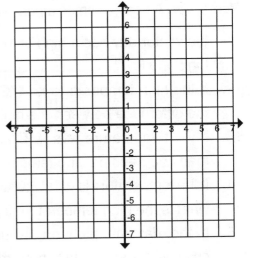

ACTIVITY 150 Logic Problems

Name:_____

Date:_____

Draw a diagram to solve this logic problem.

Five friends were watching a soccer match. They were the only ones sitting in that row of the bleachers. Becky was sitting to the right of Jake. Carol was not sitting next to Tom. Brian was not sitting next to Jake. Tom was sitting to the right of Brian. Carol was not sitting next to Jake or Brian.

1. Who was sitting next to Carol? _____

2. Tom was sitting on one side of Brian. Who was sitting on the other side?

_____

3. Which two friends were on the ends of the bench? _____

4. Which boy was sitting next to Jake? _____

5. Who was sitting in the middle? _____

ACTIVITY 151 Integers

Name:_____

Date:_____

Integers include whole numbers above and below 0 on the number line. **Negative integers** are commonly used in accounting, time lines, and in temperature readings.

Reminder: A positive times a positive is a positive, and a negative times a negative is a positive.

1. If a winter day has a high of 10°C and a low of -15°C, what is the difference between the high and low? _____

2. If the high temperature is -1°C, and the low temperature is -18°C, what is the difference between the high and low? _____

3. If the temperature was -2°C at 5:30 A.M., but it is 18°C at 12:30 P.M., how many degrees has the temperature risen? _____

4. If the temperature is -5° at 6:00 A.M., and it rises 14°C to hit its high at 1:15 P.M., what is the high temperature for the day? _____

5. If the daytime high on January 10 was -5°C, and the daytime high on July 10 was 30°C, how many times hotter was it on the July day?
_____

ACTIVITY 152 Surface Area of Rectangular Solids

Name:_____

Date:_____

To find the surface area of a 3-dimensional rectangular form, find the area of each surface and add the products together.

Jenny made props for a play. She wanted to cover several rectangular boxes with gift wrap. How many square inches of wrapping paper does she need?

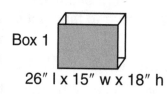

Box 1
26" l x 15" w x 18" h

Box 2
19" l x 17" w x 14" h

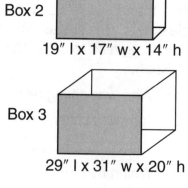

Box 3
29" l x 31" w x 20" h

1. Find the surface area of each box.

   Box 1: _____ Box 2: _____

   Box 3: _____ Box 4: _____

2. Find the total surface area for all four boxes.

   _____

3. Opposite sides of a rectangular form are congruent. Can you think of a shortcut to find the surface area? _____

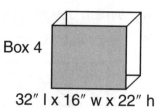

Box 4
32" l x 16" w x 22" h

76

ACTIVITY 153 Calculating Interest

Name:_____

Date:_____

Use your knowledge of percents to answer these
questions about Jared's bank account. At the end of the year, the interest is added to the total
in the account.

1. Jared has $350 in his account. On January 2, his uncle gives him
   $210 to deposit. How much money does Jared have at the beginning
   of the year? _____

2. Jared does not deposit any more money, but his money does earn 4%
   interest per year. How much interest does it earn during the year? _____

3. How much money does Jared have at the end of the year? _____

4. Jared's father matches the money in Jared's account at the end of the year. After his
   father's deposit, how much money is in Jared's account? _____

5. The bank raises its interest rate to 5% per year. How much interest will Jared earn on his
   growing account during the next year? _____

- -

ACTIVITY 154 Multiple Line Graphs

Name:_____

Date:_____

Study the graph and answer the questions.

1. How many total cans did all of the
   classes collect during week one?

   _____

2. Which class started poorly and improved?

   _____

3. Which class brought in the most cans?

   _____

4. Which classes's contributions had a mode
   of 10 cans? _____

5. Which class had a mean contribution of
   22 cans? _____

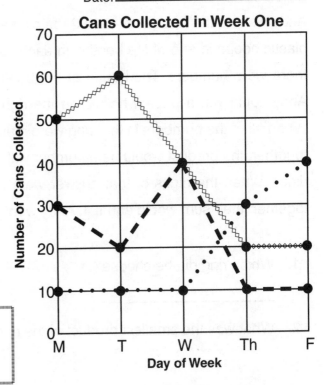

Cans Collected in Week One

Number of Cans Collected

Day of Week

· · · · Class One
⬦⬦⬦⬦⬦⬦ Class Two
▬ ▬ ▬ Class Three

77

ACTIVITY 155 Equations With Missing Operations

Name:_____

Date:_____

Thieves entered Algebraica during the night and stole all of the operations signs. In the morning, all of the equations were confused. Help them out by adding all of the missing signs. Each sign is used only once. They are $+$, $-$, $\times$, $\div$, $>$, $<$, and $=$.

1. 12 _____ 42 = 504

2. 1,836 _____ 36 = 51

3. 82 _____ 87 = 169

4. 10,892 _____ 8,211 = 2,681

5. 223 + 74 _____ 122 + 91

6. 12 x 14 _____ 100 + 90

7. 72 ÷ 12 _____ 6 x 1

ACTIVITY 156 Venn Diagrams

Name:_____

Date:_____

Andy went to the fair. There were three overlapping plastic hoops in one of the booths. In each section, there were numbers. The barker at the booth said Andy could win a prize if he picked the right ring. When all of the numbers in that ring were multiplied together, the product would be a number with three digits. When the digits of that answer were added together, their sum would equal 4. Andy won!

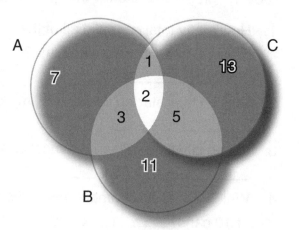

1. Which ring did he choose?

_____

2. What was the smallest product of the numbers in the rings? _____

ACTIVITY 157 Add and Round Off Large Numbers

Name: _____

Date: _____

In 2006, the populations of Canada's three largest metropolitan areas were recorded as part of the nation's census. Toronto had the most people, with a population of 5,113,149. Montreal was the second most populous city, with 3,635,571 residents. Vancouver ranked third, with 2,116,581 people living there.

1. How many people were living in the two largest metropolitan areas? Round off your answer to the nearest thousand. _____

2. How many people were living in Montreal and Vancouver? Round off to the nearest ten thousand. _____

3. How many people were living in all three metropolitan areas? Round off your answer to the nearest hundred thousand. _____

4. Round off the population of each city to the nearest million. _____,

_____, _____

> **Census Form**   **Canada**
> 1. How many people live in this home, apartment, or mobile home?
> ☐ Number of people
> INCLUDE: Foster children, housemates, boarders and temporary workers.
> DO NOT INCLUDE: Students living away, overseas military, people in institutions, nursing home, or jails.

ACTIVITY 158 Multiply and Round-Off Decimals

Name: _____

Date: _____

About 5,113,149 people lived in the Toronto metropolitan area in 2006.

1. If 0.6 of the people in Toronto bought a new book about the city's history, how many books would be sold? Round off to the nearest whole number. _____

2. If 0.04 of the people in Toronto visited a website once, how many times would it be visited by Toronto residents? Round off to the nearest whole number. _____

3. If 0.001 of the people in Toronto attended a festival, how many would attend? Round off to the nearest whole number.

_____

ACTIVITY 159 Exponents

Name:_____

Date:_____

Exponents tell you how many times to multiply a number by itself.

Example: 5 x 5 x 5 is 5^3.

Danny's mother had a birthday party yesterday. Danny asked her how old she was, and she hesitated.

1. Finally, she said that she was 2^5 years old. How old was she? _____

2. Danny's older brother said he was 2^4 years old. How old was he? _____

3. Danny's younger brother said he was 3^2 years old. How old was he? _____

4. If Danny is $2^3 + 2^2$ years old, how old is he? _____

ACTIVITY 160 Reducing Fractions

Name:_____

Date:_____

Reducing fractions to their lowest terms sometimes takes several steps. To save time, find the greatest common factor for the numerator and denominator. Multiplication practice will help you recognize factors more quickly. Read the questions and reduce the fractions to their lowest terms.

After the family reunion, Andy helped his cousin gather up the food remaining on the tables.

1. Originally, there had been 144 chocolate chip cookies. There were 16 chocolate chip cookies left, or $\frac{16}{144}$ of the total. Reduce the fraction to its lowest terms. _____

2. There were 49 butter cookies left. Originally, there had been 98 butter cookies. $\frac{49}{98}$ were left. Reduce the fraction to its lowest terms. _____

3. Originally, there were 160 oz. of punch. The boys found that 32 oz. of punch were left. That was $\frac{32}{160}$, or _____.

4. Originally, there had been 125 paper cups. When the boys put the remaining cups back into the box, they found 50. That was $\frac{50}{125}$, or _____.

80

ACTIVITY 161 Changing Fractions to Decimals

Name: _____

Date: _____

To change a fraction to a decimal, divide the numerator by the denominator.

1. Jake wanted to check some fraction problems with his calculator, but when he tried, he discovered that the device showed only decimals. To check his answers, he had to change each fraction into a decimal. His first answer was $\frac{5}{12}$. How would $\frac{5}{12}$ appear on his calculator screen? Round off the result to the nearest thousandth. _____

2. What was special about the number? _____

_____

3. Which is a more exact representation of the quantity, $\frac{5}{12}$ or 0.417? _____

   Give a reason for your answer. _____

4. What are the advantages of using decimal fractions? _____

_____

- -

ACTIVITY 162 Factor Trees

Name: _____

Date: _____

Jan made a factor tree to find the prime factors for 192.
Unfortunately, she left her paper on the patio, and some of the numbers were washed away.

1. Write the missing numbers on the diagram.

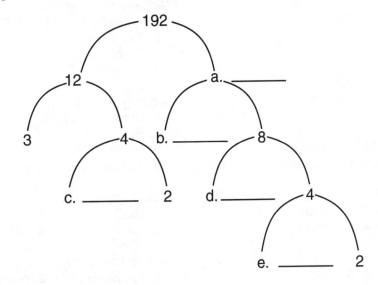

2. List the prime factorization of 192. _____

Answer Keys

Activity 1 (p. 1)
1. 4 lines: 62 in line 1, 60 in line 2, 56 in line 3, 59 in line 4
2. spiny lobsters
3. Answers will vary.
4. Answers will vary.

Activity 2 (p. 1)
1. up to 20 per burrow: 12 in 1st burrow, 6 in 2nd, 11 in 3rd, 20 in 4th
2. iguana eggs
3. Answers will vary.
4. Answers will vary
5. Answers will vary.

Activity 3 (p. 2)
1. 3   2. 6
3. 2   4. 1
5. 4

Activity 4 (p. 2)
1. row 2
2. 12 pepper plants
3. 17 corn plants
4. 5 watermelon plants
5. She grew more beefsteak tomatoes.

Activity 5 (p. 3)
1. 553 points   2. 425 points
3. 324 points   4. 776 points
5. Mike and Jared

Activity 6 (p. 3)
1. 995 cans   2. 1,152 cans
3. 1,344 cans   4. 885 cans
5. Jeremy and Jordan

Activity 7 (p. 4)
1. 278 books   2. 128 books
3. 118 books   4. 468 books

Activity 8 (p. 4)
1. 836 sheets   2. 633 sheets
3. 612 sheets   4. 512 sheets

Activity 9 (p. 5)
1. 262 spiders   2. 281 spiders
3. 293 spiders   4. 370 spiders

Activity 10 (p. 5)
1. 494 pictures   2. 518 pictures
3. 723 pictures   4. 337 pictures

Activity 11 (p. 6)
1. 816 stamps   2. 73 stamps
3. 456 stamps   4. 209 stamps

Activity 12 (p. 6)
1. 104 bottles   2. 38 bottles
3. 97 bottles   4. 30 bottles

Activity 13 (p. 7)
1. 237 cans of garbanzo beans
2. 1,018 cans of beans
3. 103 cans of black beans
4. 818 cans of navy and black beans

Activity 14 (p. 7)
1. *How many more, than,* 129 tomatoes
2. *How many, in all,* 635 vegetables
3. *How many, in all,* 399 vegetables
4. *How many more, than,* 209 cilantro bunches

Activity 15 (p. 8)
1. *Lady's Life*
2. a men's golf tournament
3. the boys' department

Activity 16 (p. 8)
1. 920 book jackets for nonfiction; 460 book jackets for picture books
2. 6 bookcases for fiction; 5 bookcases for picture books
3. reference
4. 600 fiction books

Activity 17 (p. 9)
1. Angel Falls and Tugela Falls
2. Tugela Falls and Monge Falls
3. Tugela Falls
4. 9,000 ft.

Activity 18 (p. 9)
1. Chang Jiang River
2. Huang He River
3. Ob River
4. Amazon River

Activity 19 (p. 10)
1. Lot C   2. 66 cars
3. Lot A   4. 168 cars

Activity 20 (p. 10)
1. 150 pears   2. peach jam
3. no   4. 156 apricots

Activity 21 (p. 11)
1. 348 strips of red paper
2. 522 strips of orange paper
3. 273 gold stars
4. They used 195 silver stars, so one box of 200 was enough.

Activity 22 (p. 11)
1. 2,216 trees   2. 1,820 trees
3. They needed 1,794 trees, so 1,800 seedlings were enough.
4. 2,163 trees

Activity 23 (p. 12)
1. 12 ladybird beetles
2. 18 beagles
3. 36 basketball players
4. nine teams of horses

Activity 24 (p. 12)
1. 10 cookies   2. 18 scoops
3. 30 spoonfuls   4. 45 faces

Activity 25 (p. 13)
1. 18 apples per bag with 3 left over
2. 30 apples per box with 3 left over
3. 46 pairs with 1 apple left over
4. 23 pies with 1 apple left over

Activity 26 (p. 13)
1. 11 books in each box and 1 book in the envelope
2. 44 books per shelf with 1 left over
3. the ninth day
4. 8 books left

Activity 27 (p. 14)
1. 25 pieces of trash   2. 50 pieces of trash
3. 100 pieces of trash   4. 40 points

Activity 28 (p. 14)
1. 86 sixth graders   2. 172 pencils
3. 43 pencils   4. 4 bags of pencils

Activity 29 (p. 15)
1. 512 students   2. 1 pass
3. 640 packets   4. 1 pass

Activity 30 (p. 15)
1. 578 families   2. 1 coupon
3. 321 coupons   4. 564 coupons
5. 96 coupons   6. 753 coupons

Activity 31 (p. 16)
1. 42 cards   2. 42 x 5 = 210
3. 52 cards with 2 left over
4. 52 x 4 = 208 + 2 = 210

Activity 32 (p. 16)
1. 41 cupcakes   2. 41 x 5 = 205
3. 29 cupcakes with 2 candies left over
4. 29 x 7 = 203 + 2 = 205

Activity 33 (p. 17)
1. 17 children   2. 36 kits
3. 12 children   4. 5 children

Activity 34 (p. 17)
1. 17 tables   2. 11 students
3. 16 students   4. 6 students

Activity 35 (p. 18)
1. 3 points   2. 4 points
3. 4 points   4. improve

Activity 36 (p. 18)
1. 90   2. 85
3. 87.5   4. 88

Activity 37 (p. 19)
1. b   2. b
3. d   4. a

Activity 38 (p. 19)
1. 84   2. 84
3. 80   4. 81
5. yes, their average score on quiz 5 was 81

Activity 39 (p. 20)
1. D   2. A
3. B   4. C

Activity 40 (p. 20)
1. triangle   2. rectangle
3. hexagon   4. ray
5. line

Activity 41 (p. 21)
1. right   2. acute
3. obtuse   4. right

Activity 42 (p. 21)
1. right   2. acute
3. obtuse   4. 5
5. 2   6. 4

Activity 43 (p. 22)
1. radius
2. diameter
3. center
4. ED, EA, and EB

Activity 44 (p. 22)
1. a circle
2. a radius
3. You are in the center of a circle.
4. an infinite number

Activity 45 (p. 23)
1. A̶ B̶ C̶ D̶ E̶ H̶ I̶ M̶ O̶ T̶ U̶ V̶ W̶ X̶ Y̶
2. H
3.

Activity 46 (p. 23)
1.

2. Answers will vary. Should include two Es.

Activity 47 (p. 24)
1. D
2. B and G
3. C
4. F

Activity 48 (p. 24)
1. B
2. E
3. D
4. A and C do not fit.

Activity 49 (p. 25)
1. five, B
2. five, D
3. C
4. A

Activity 50 (p. 25)
1. D
2. A
3. E
4. C
5. B

Activity 51 (p. 26)
1. Bill
2. Grace
3. Allen
4. Armando
Challenge: Grace

Activity 52 (p. 26)
1. Marcus
2. Heather and Liv
3. Marcus
4. one hour

Activity 53 (p. 27)

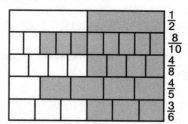

1. Tuesday, Wednesday, Thursday
2. Monday and Friday

Activity 54 (p. 27)

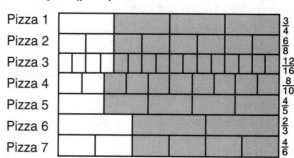

1. 3
2. 2

Activity 55 (p. 28)

1. $\frac{1}{4}$, $\frac{2}{8}$, $\frac{4}{16}$, yes

Activity 56 (p. 28)
1. $\frac{9}{12}$, $\frac{12}{16}$, $\frac{15}{20}$, $\frac{18}{24}$, $\frac{21}{28}$, $\frac{24}{32}$, $\frac{27}{36}$
2. $\frac{60}{80}$, $\frac{90}{120}$, $\frac{120}{160}$, $\frac{150}{200}$, $\frac{180}{240}$, $\frac{210}{280}$, $\frac{240}{320}$, $\frac{270}{360}$
3. $\frac{60}{80}$, $\frac{75}{100}$

Activity 57 (p. 29)
1. $\frac{12}{28}$ or $\frac{3}{7}$
2. $\frac{24}{28}$ or $\frac{6}{7}$
3. $\frac{16}{28}$ or $\frac{4}{7}$
4. $\frac{16}{28}$ or $\frac{4}{7}$

Activity 58 (p. 29)
1. $\frac{12}{32}$ or $\frac{3}{8}$ 2. $\frac{20}{32}$ or $\frac{5}{8}$
3. $\frac{25}{32}$ 4. $\frac{22}{32}$ or $\frac{11}{16}$

Activity 59 (p. 30)
1. $\frac{6}{8}$ or $\frac{3}{4}$ of a cup   2. $\frac{3}{8}$ of a cup
3. $\frac{1}{8}$ of a cup   4. yes

Activity 60 (p. 30)
1. $\frac{13}{24}$ 2. $\frac{3}{24}$
3. $\frac{1}{24}$

Activity 61 (p. 31)
1. $2\frac{1}{6}$ 2. $1\frac{1}{2}$
3. $3\frac{1}{4}$ 4. $\frac{2}{3}$

Activity 62 (p. 31)
1. $1\frac{1}{12}$ 2. $2\frac{2}{15}$
3. $1\frac{13}{20}$ 4. $\frac{3}{4}$

Activity 63 (p. 32)
1. $\frac{52}{24}$ 2. $\frac{30}{24}$
3. $\frac{73}{24}$ 4. $\frac{32}{24}$

Activity 64 (p. 32)
1. $\frac{113}{36}$ 2. $\frac{82}{36}$
3. $\frac{146}{36}$ 4. $\frac{181}{36}$

Activity 65 (p. 33)
1. 3 sandwiches   2. $2\frac{3}{4}$ km, $5\frac{1}{2}$ km
3. $2\frac{1}{2}$ hours   4. 1 hour. Answers will vary.

Activity 66 (p. 33)
1. $6\frac{1}{2}$ hours   2. 8 hours
3. 12 hours   4. 6 P.M.

Activity 67 (p. 34)
1. 0.6   2. 0.7
3. 0.3   4. 0.07

Activity 68 (p. 34)
1. 0.08   2. 0.05
3. 0.42

Activity 69 (p. 35)
1. 46.9 cm   2. 77.5 cm
3. 64.1 cm   4. 48.4 cm

Activity 70 (p. 35)
1. 7.67 kg   2. 1.02 kg
3. 5.73 kg   4. 5.63 kg

Activity 71 (p. 36)
1. $\frac{1}{2}$ 2. $\frac{1}{4}$
3. 0.6   4. 0.7

Activity 72 (p. 36)
1. $\frac{1}{3}$ 2. 0.75
3. $\frac{18}{20}$ 4. 0.67

Activity 73 (p. 37)
1. Tuesday   2. Wednesday and Friday
3. 30°   4. 42°

Activity 74 (p. 37)
1. Manuel   2. Denise
3. 80   4. 500
5. 125

Activity 75 (p. 38)
1. grilled cheese   2. sliced beef
3. roast turkey   4. 100 students

Activity 76 (p. 38)
1. apples   2. ants on a log
3. 45   4. 30

Activity 77 (p. 39)
1. 1:10   2. 4:10
3. 2:10   4. 3:10
5. 9:10

Activity 78 (p. 39)
1. 12:250 or 6:125   2. 233:250
3. 225:250 or 9:10   4. 50:250 or 1:5

Activity 79 (p. 40)
1. a tree   2. a telephone/electric pole
3. a fence   4. a birdbath
5. in a park

Activity 80 (p. 40)
1. a picnic table   2. a rock
3. a water fountain   4. a bench
5. a basketball hoop   6. her ring

Activity 81 (p. 41)
1. 12 outfits

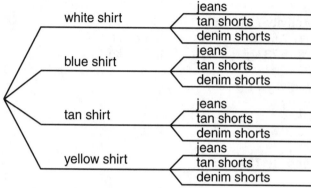

2. 1:12

Activity 82 (p. 41)
1:15. Diagrams will vary.

Activity 83 (p. 42)
1. 27 in.   2. 2 ft. 3 in.
3. 4 ft. board   4. 1 ft. 9 in.

Activity 84 (p. 42)
1. 56 in.
2. $1\frac{20}{36}$, 1 yard and 20 inches, or $1\frac{5}{9}$ yards
3. 2-yard length   4. 1 ft. 4 in.

Activity 85 (p. 43)
1. 18 cm   2. 12 cm
3. 45 cm   4. 15 cm
5. no

Activity 86 (p. 43)
1. 230 cm or 2.3 m   2. 60 cm
3. 40 cm   4. Amanda's
5. 57.5 cm

Activity 87 (p. 44)
1. 1,760 yds.   2. 2 miles
3. 3,080 yds.   4. 880 more yards
Challenge: $330

Activity 88 (p. 44)
1. Morgan   2. Terry
3. 1,320 yards   4. 3,960 feet

Activity 89 (p. 45)
1. 150,000 m   2. 30,000 m
3. 1,500 m   4. 7,350 m

Activity 90 (p. 45)
1. eight and eighty-five hundredths kilometers
2. eight and four hundred sixty-three thousandths kilometers
3. two hundred thirty-nine meters
4. seventy meters

Activity 91 (p. 46)
1. 320 squares   2. 72 ft.
3. 24 yds.   4. 160 sq. ft.

Activity 92 (p. 46)
1. 50 m   2. 154 sq. m or 154 m^2
3. 2 sq. m or 2 m^2 4. 6 m

Activity 93 (p. 47)
1. 1 cubic ft. or 1 ft.^{3} 2. 12 blocks
3. 8 blocks   4. C

Activity 94 (p. 47)
1. 306,000 cubic centimeters or cm^3
2. 1,000,000 cm^3
3. B. They would have topsoil left over.

   $\frac{1}{2}$ cubic meter = 500,000 cubic cm, which is more than 306,000 cubic centimeters.
4. 1,285,350 cubic centimeters.
5. all in one trip

Activity 95 (p. 48)
1. basketballs   2. 50 oz., $3\frac{1}{8}$ lbs.
3. a soccer team   4. 8 balls
5. 43 oz.; $2\frac{11}{16}$ lbs.; or 2 lbs., 11 oz.

Activity 96 (p. 48)
1. 4 apples   2. 20 apples
3. 8,000 apples   4. 12 ounces of apples

Activity 97 (p. 49)
1. 112,000 g   2. 8 kg
3. 12,000 g   4. 132 kg

Activity 98 (p. 49)
1. 236,000 kg   2. 240,000 kg; 240 t
3. 440,000 kg; 440 t   4. no; yes
Challenge: 12.2 metric tons

86

Activity 99 (p. 50)
1. 45 minutes
2. 15 minutes
3. $1\frac{1}{2}$ hrs.
4. 1 hour
5. 30 minutes
6. $2\frac{1}{2}$ hrs.

Activity 100 (p. 50)
1. 3 hours 20 minutes
2. 1 hour 30 minutes
3. 1 hour 20 minutes
4. 35 minutes
5. 25 minutes

Activity 101 (p. 51)
1. 60 minutes or 1 hour
2. 3 hours
3. 120 miles
4. 2 P.M.

Activity 102 (p. 51)
1. $\frac{1}{2}$ hour, 0.5 hr., or 30 minutes
2. $\frac{1}{6}$ of an hour or 10 minutes
3. $\frac{3}{4}$ of an hour or 45 minutes
4. 1 hour or 60 minutes

Activity 103 (p. 52)
1. 11:20 A.M.
2. 12:05 P.M.
3. 8:10 A.M.
4. 10:00 A.M.

Activity 104 (p. 52)
1. 9:00 A.M.
2. 7:00 P.M.
3. 5:00 P.M.
4. 8:00 A.M.

Activity 105 (p.53)
1. 50 dimes
2. 200 nickels
3. 80 quarters
4. 500 pennies
5. Answers will vary, but coin values must total 50 cents, and three different coins must be included in each combination.

Activity 106 (p. 53)
1. 20 dimes
2. 20 quarters
3. 20 nickels
4. Answers will vary. All combinations should equal $2.

Activity 107 (p. 54)
1. $6
2. $3, $9
3. $8
4. $18.03
5. $1.03
6. yes

Activity 108 (p. 54)
1. $9
2. $8
3. Pete: $11; Andrew $12
4. Pete: $8.97; Andrew: $7.66

Activity 109 (p. 55)
1. $205.73
2. $3.05
3. $524.46
4. $1,030.76
5. $2,061.52

Activity 110 (p. 55)
1. $1,127.20
2. $347.88
3. $1,582.20
4. $117.80

Activity 111 (p. 56)
1. $4.45
2. $5.97
3. $11.40
4. $12.75

Activity 112 (p. 56)
1. $14.01
2. $53.82
3. $16.25
4. $12.60
5. No, sold separately, the pencils and box would cost only $14.60.
6. $3.32

Activity 113 (p. 57)
1. $35.20
2. $5.25
3. $2.99
4. $56.18

Activity 114 (p. 57)
1. $4.05
2. $2.49
3. $1.30
4. $9.38
5. $11.45; $2.29

Activity 115 (p. 58)
1. 518,420,000 cubic feet
2. 1,837,440 feet long
3. 1,788 feet deeper
4. 2,258 feet deeper

Activity 116 (p. 58)
1. 2,624,895 km^2
2. 1,621.25 m
3. South China Sea
4. 915 m

Activity 117 (p. 59)
1. 126 bags
2. 132 bags
3. 199 bags
4. Davis Street

Activity 118 (p. 59)
1. 15 books
2. 5 textbooks
3. 25 sheets
4. $25.68

Activity 119 (p. 60)
1. 23
2. 25
3. 16
4. 115
5. 841
Challenge: Answers will vary.

Activity 120 (p. 60)

1. 860.4 or $860\frac{2}{5}$
2. *Mark Anders, Middle School Detective,* and *Talent Incorporated*
3. 316, *Dear Andrea*
4. 2007, Some are more popular than others. The results are not close.
5. 4,302

Challenge: Answers will vary, but could include that they would want to advertise on the more popular programs.

Activity 121 (p. 61)

1. $\frac{3}{4}$
2. $\frac{3}{8}$
3. $\frac{5}{6}$
4. $\frac{5}{8}$

Activity 122 (p. 61)

1. $\frac{5}{12}$
2. 3 pieces of board B, 6 pieces of board D, 4 pieces of board D plus 1 piece of board B, 1 piece of board A plus one piece of board B
3. 1 piece of board A, 2 pieces of board B, 3 pieces of board C, 4 pieces of board D, 1 piece of board C plus 2 pieces of board D
4. Answers will vary. 2 pieces of board B or 1 piece of board A

Activity 123 (p. 62)

1. $\frac{3}{4}$ more sandwiches
2. $1\frac{1}{8}$ more sandwiches
3. $6\frac{1}{4}$ sandwiches
4. $8\frac{5}{8}$ sandwiches
5. $6\frac{3}{8}$ sandwiches

Activity 124 (p. 62)

1. $5\frac{2}{3}$ pies
2. $3\frac{1}{4}$ more apple pies
3. $8\frac{1}{4}$ pies
4. $3\frac{11}{12}$ peach and cherry pies

Activity 125 (p. 63)

1. $8\frac{1}{2}$ feet
2. $4\frac{3}{8}$ square feet
3. $1\frac{1}{4}$ feet
4. $\frac{1}{16}$ square feet
5. $4\frac{7}{16}$ square feet

Activity 126 (p. 63)

1. $49\frac{1}{2}$ ft.
2. $148\frac{5}{8}$ square feet
3. $34\frac{3}{8}$ square feet
4. $14\frac{1}{16}$ square feet
5. $197\frac{1}{16}$ square feet

Activity 127 (p. 64)

1. 10 e-mails
2. $2\frac{1}{2}$ levels
3. $3\frac{3}{4}$ reviews
4. 5 friends

Activity 128 (p. 64)

1. $8\frac{2}{3}$ squares
2. 13 squares
3. $14\frac{3}{4}$ squares
4. $11\frac{4}{5}$ squares

Activity 129 (p. 65)

1. 126 students, 14 students
2. 8 students
3. 34 students
4. 42 seventh-graders

Activity 130 (p. 65)

1. $164.75
2. $12.77
3. $1,560.00
4. $1,416.00

Activity 131 (p. 66)

1. 26 cups
2. 3.61 pitchers
3. 6.84 bottles
4. 18.57 glasses

Activity 132 (p. 66)

1. 25.25 bows
2. 6.16 gifts
3. 7.77 necklaces
4. 101 magnets

Activity 133 (p. 67)

1. 40%
2. 100%
3. 83%
4. 83%
5. 77%
6. C

Activity 134 (p. 67)

1. 26%
2. 43%
3. 77%
4. 88%
5. Leo

Activity 135 (p. 68)

1. 25:50, 50:100, or 100:200
2. 10:15, 20:30, or 30:45
3. 50:10, 5:1, or 100:20
4. 15:25, 30:50, 60:100

Activity 136 (p. 68)
1. 40:100, 2:5, 4:10
2. 40:60, 2:3, or 4:6
3. 30:100, 3:10, or 6:20
4. 60:100, 6:10, 12:20

Activity 137 (p. 69)
1. 40 cm   2. 30 cm
3. 4 cm   4. 6 cm

Activity 138 (p. 69)
1. 7   2. 10
3. 20   4. 60

Activity 139 (p. 70)
1. a cone   2. a cube
3. a square pyramid   4. a sphere
5. a circle when lying down and a rectangle when
   standing
   The bases are circles, and the side is a rectangle.

Activity 140 (p. 70)
1. a cube   2. a square pyramid
3. an octahedron   4. a triangular prism

Activity 141 (p. 71)
1. 188.4 cm   2. 125.6 cm
3. 282.6 cm   4. 251.2 cm
5. 847.8 cm or 8.478 m

Activity 142 (p. 71)
1. 157 m   2. 37.68 m
3. 157 cm or 1.57 m
Challenge: 3 m

Activity 143 (p. 72)
1. 60 square feet   2. 96 square feet
3. 30 square feet   4. 160 square feet

Activity 144 (p. 72)
1. 72 square feet   2. 12 square feet
3. 18 square feet   4. 102 square feet

Activity 145 (p. 73)
1. 77 ants   2. 7 more flies
3. 21 more bees   4. 189 insects
5. 11:5 or 77:35   6. 4/5 = 28/35

Activity 146 (p. 73)
1. 60 paper clips   2. 150 tacks
3. 30 more pencils   4. 5:2 or 150:60
5. 300

Activity 147 (p. 74)
1. 22 students   2. 3
3. 5.5   4. 5.5
5. 7:6
6. Individual sports to family activities (in that order)

Activity 148 (p. 74)
1. 22,333 readers   2. 3,169
3. 8,462   4. 7,444.33
5. No. Explanations will vary.

Activity 149 (p. 75)
2. The figure is an X.
Challenge: Answers will vary.

Activity 150 (p. 75)
Correct order as viewed from behind the bench:
Carol, Becky, Jake, Tom, Brian
1. Becky   2. nobody
3. Carol and Brian   4. Tom
5. Jake

Activity 151 (p. 76)
1. 25°   2. 17°
3. 20°   4. 9°C
5. 7 times hotter

Activity 152 (p. 76)
1. Box 1: 2,256 square inches
   Box 2: 1,654 square inches
   Box 3: 4,198 square inches
   Box 4: 3,136 square inches
2. 11,244 square inches
3. surface area = (perimeter x height) + (2 x base)
   Exact formulas will vary.

Activity 153 (p. 77)
1. $560   2. $22.40
3. $582.40   4. $1,164.80
5. $58.24

Activity 154 (p. 77)
1. 400 cans   2. Class One
3. Class Two
4. Class One and Three   5. Class Three

Activity 155 (p. 78)
1. x   2. ÷
3. +   4. −
5. >   6. <
7. =

Activity 156 (p. 78)
1. C   2. A = 42

Activity 157 (p. 79)
1. 8,749,000 people
2. 5,750,000 people
3. 10,900,000 people
4. Toronto: 5,000,000 people
   Montreal 4,000,000 people
   Vancouver 2,000,000 people

Activity 158 (p. 79)
1. 3,067,889 books   2. 204,526 visits
3. 5,113 attendees

Activity 159 (p. 80)
1. 32 years old   2. 16 years old
3. 9 years old   4. 12 years old

Activity 160 (p. 80)

1. $\frac{1}{9}$ 2. $\frac{1}{2}$

3. $\frac{1}{5}$ 4. $\frac{2}{5}$

Activity 161 (p. 81)
1. 0.417   2. the six kept repeating

3. $\frac{5}{12}$; Answers will vary.   4. Answers will vary.

Activity 162 (p. 81)
1. a. 16   b. 2   c. 2
   d. 2   e. 2
2. 2 x 2 x 2 x 2 x 2 x 2 x 3